Oh, That's Another Story

Images and Tales of Sag Harbor

Oh, That's Another Story
Images and Tales of Sag Harbor

By Alexandra Eames

Paintings by Whitney Brooks Hansen

Harbor Electronic Publishing
| Sag Harbor, New York |
HEPDigital.com
2015

Text © 2015 by Alexandra Eames

Images © 2015 by Whitney Brooks Hansen

Library of Congress Control Number: 2015937690

ISBN 978-1-932916-18-8 (paper)

ISBN 978-1-932916-19-5 (eBook)

All rights reserved. No part of this publication may be reproduced, stored in a retrieval system, or transmitted in any form or by any means without the prior permission of Harbor Electronic Publishing. Permission is granted to photocopy any part of the book under contract with the Copyright Clearance Center (copyright.com).

Printed in the United States of America.

First printing: June 2015

A Note on the Type: *Oh, That's Another Story* is set in Minion Pro, an Adobe Originals typeface designed by Robert Slimbach. It was inspired by classical, old-style typefaces of the late Renaissance, a period of elegant, beautiful, and highly readable type designs. The caption font is Gill Sans. Designed by Eric Gill, it is the Helvetica of England; ubiquitous and utilitarian.

Village of Sag Harbor, NY

1 Long Wharf, 2 Bay Street Theatre, 3 Sag Harbor Yacht Club, 4 Breakwater Yacht Club, 5 Cormaria, 6 Havens Beach, 7 Eastville, 8 St. David Church, 9 Temple Adas Israel, 10 Christ Church, 11 Bulova Factory, 12 Umbrella House, 13 St. Andrew Church, 14 Old Whalers' Church, 15 Old Burying Ground, 16 Firemen's Museum, 17 American Hotel, 18 Sag Harbor Historical Society, 19 John Jermain Memorial Library, 20 Whaling Museum, 21 Custom House, 22 Upper Cove, 23 Otter Pond, 24 Oakland Cemetery, 25 Mashashimuet Park, 26 Tomato Lady's Stand, 27 Canio's Books.

TO THE PEOPLE OF SAG HARBOR

For their knowledge and stories we thank:

Fred Abelman
Miles B. Anderson
Patricia A. Archibald
Nada D. Barry
David E. Bray
Margaret Abelman Bromberg
Michael S. Bromberg
Robert P. Browngardt
Philip J. Bucking
Lawrence J. Burns Jr.
Joseph Burns
Michael A. Butler
Joan T. Carlson
JoAnne W. Carter
Anita Cilli
John M. Cilli
Ana R. Daniel
John Russell Eberhardt
Olin Edwards
Mary Lee Egusquiza
James Federico
Susan Field
Barbara Fiore
Doris Gronlund
Maria "Mia" Grosjean
Anne Hansen
Deborah Smythe Jacobs
Robert L. Jacobs

May Kelman
David Lee
Joy Lewis
Rocco Liccardi
Claude R. "Bob" Maeder
Sister Ann Marino, RSHM
Marie Schiavoni Mangano
Jane Bennett Markowski
Joseph F. Markowski Sr.
Elinor McDade
Carol Olejnik
William Pickens III
Brenda Ward Ploeger
Lovelady Powell
Craig Rhodes
Diane Pintavalle Schiavoni
George "Gabe" Schiavoni
Victoria Schiavoni
Dorothy Sherry
Kathy Tucker
Marty Trunzo
Jack van Kovics
John A. Ward
The Rev. Shawn Williams
Sharon York
Jack Youngs
Dorothy I. Zaykowski

Contents

Preface	11
Introduction	13
1 Neighborhoods	15
2 Religions	25
3 Industry	35
4 Farms	43
5 Shops and Businesses	49
6 Gas Stations	65
7 Bars and Restaurants	69
8 Cinema and Theater	75
9 Social Clubs, Civic Organizations, Fire Department	81
10 Schools	93
11 Library, Book Stores, and Newspapers	101
12 Antique Shops and Art Galleries	107
Historical Timeline	115
Acknowledgments	121
Bibliography	125
About the Author and Artist	127

Preface

I was born and raised on the upper west side of Manhattan—in a nice old 1930s building, had apartments on the lower east side, lived on an island near Seattle, in rural Pennsylvania, in downtown Seattle, and, for six years, in a Paris apartment in the Marais. From there, I got to Sag Harbor, and Sag Harbor got to me.

A village turned out to be my perfect place—I explain to friends, "I go to the post office and I'm there for fifteen minutes." Ditto Schiavoni's wonderful grocery store. The time spent talking, saying hello, and it occurs to me now that I know, a little or a lot, dozens of people.

This is not paradise. In the summertime, the lawn mowers and the leaf blowers never quit. I once ran to the window in a fury at the sound of lawn mowers. Mowing, as it happened, my lawn. Deer eat your plants, And, May 31 to Labor Day, *people*. My parking strategies here are better than the ones I used in Paris, but sometimes it looks like you just have to go back to your house without whatever it was.

Still, I'm home. The custom here is to hold doors, and when one person says "Thank-you" the other always answers "You're welcome." That's everybody: artists, contractors, the guys who mow the lawns, the nuns from the convent. So, I'm hooked, here for life, and I think the following pages will give you some idea why.

—Alan Furst

Introduction

Oh, *That's Another Story: Images and Tales of Sag Harbor* recalls the memories of a 300-year-old industrial village and the inevitable waves of change that have forged a strong, resilient, sometimes raucous community. Sag Harbor is well loved by its residents and by vacationers who make it their second home. Five wars, four catastrophic fires, and recurring economic booms and busts have been met with persistence, goodwill, and the quick wit of local inhabitants. Over the long haul their efforts, individual mores and cultures have blended to create an environment that is diverse, respectful of tradition, and at the same time tolerant of strangers and new ideas.

With paintings of twentieth-century scenes and the daily banter of a lively community, we present the backstory of this lively village. Sag Harbor's tales are offered in the words of those we interviewed and are based on their personal memories. Every story has another version, one that has evolved and been embellished over decades of telling, and will be told again and again in new ways. We have heard other versions of some of these tales but honor and quote the people we talked to in person.

Our first thought of a book about Sag Harbor came to Whitney and me on a walk around our village. We were chatting about the amusing stories we had heard over the years and the fact that many of them might disappear as Sag Harbor, the gritty factory town, evolved into an upscale resort in the twenty-first century. In the next minute we had decided to collect as many of these tales by interviewing our friends and neighbors and combining them with Whitney's paintings in a book.

Whitney Hansen has been painting scenes of Sag Harbor since she came here in 1965. Her technique starts with a woodcut. The basic shapes are carved into a pine board and then colors are applied to each

Oh, That's Another Story

area. While the colors are still wet the design is printed on a sheet of textured rice paper, the grain of the wood leaving wavy patterns on the inked paper. The print is hung to dry on clotheslines strung about her studio. Whitney then adds color, texture and detail using fine brushes and oils and the print becomes a painting. The results are informal images of everyday life laid down in rich colors and layered texture. This loose, impressionistic style expresses the quirky character and patina of the rough factory buildings, small shops and old wooden houses of this three-hundred-year-old village.

Over the course of five years we have conducted fifty formal interviews with Sag Harbor residents, written and received emails, and listened well while in line at the post office. During several conversations a spouse or family member joined us and in a few instances we talked to groups of two or more people who were good friends. Sag Harborites are great talkers and sometimes the stories overlapped, which prompted more tales. They are generous, happy to tell us just about anything.

Well, not quite. If we touched on an unpleasant family spat, mentioned serious crimes, or scandal, the eyes would roll and we were met with, "Oh, that's another story." And the people of Sag Harbor are gracious, not just granting us time and faith, but also lunch or tea. It is their spirit and generosity that sustained the community through hard times, their cleverness and ingenuity that ensured the village's survival. It is their legacy that people from elsewhere—from "away"—find so welcoming and it is their hard work that made Sag Harbor what it is today.

Alexandra Eames

Sag Harbor NY

June 2015

1

Neighborhoods

In the 1980s, a well respected mason, Larry Burns, came to our house to pour a new concrete floor for our back shed. A tall, strong man with an easy smile, he is full of stories. He told us that his Uncle Billy entered a contest, "$5 for somebody who could walk the whole length of Long Wharf carrying a big barrel of oil weighing 250 pounds. He won it." Lately it has been a pleasure to see Larry out and about getting exercise, probably perusing the many sidewalks he has built in this village. Larry lived most of his life in the same neighborhood. His Irish grandfather, Joseph Burns, was born in Brooklyn and was a mason. In the 1880s when Joseph was eighteen, Mr. Fahys asked him to come to work at his new watchcase factory in Sag Harbor. "He had to get permission from his mother," Larry said.

Later Joseph married Mary Keating. They prospered and built a house on an empty lot across from her parents' home. "My grandfather Joseph poured the first sidewalks in Sag Harbor, he formed the first baseball team, and had the first telephone," recalled Larry. "He was a chemical man. He carried a gun with him since he had very critical materials they used in the watch factory. He had a good job."

Oh, That's Another Story

Jermain Avenue at Hampton Street

Larry's grandparents on his mother's side were Italian. His grandmother, Cecilia, came from Italy as a girl and worked in the family vegetable store on Washington Street. "Someone said, 'I gotta nice Italian man in Italy. Gonna bring him over to show you.' She's all dressed up and waiting to meet him. Here comes this little guy, Andy Quatroche, with flowers in his hand. She says, 'Whosa this?' 'This is the boyfriend.' 'Oh, no. He's too little!' She throws the flowers and hits him on the head with them. She ended up marrying him."

For more than one hundred years the Burns family has moved about their neighborhood but seldom more than two blocks from this corner. Larry Burns's sister lives now in Joseph Burns's house, shown here all dressed up for the Fourth of July. In the backyard the outbuildings and a grape arbor are much the same as when the house was built. The house was a gathering place, across the narrow side street from a busy grocery store. Larry's grandmother lived to be 99, saw and knew everyone that passed by, and often invited them for a bite to eat. Her next-door neighbor, Len Roberts, had no running water or electricity so she cooked his meals for him.

"Len lived to be a 100 years old. He was a walking encyclopedia. His father was carrying him on his shoulders down Bay Street when Sag Harbor burned up. It must have been in the 1880s," added Larry. Checking the history of Sag Harbor's many catastrophic fires, I find reference to one in 1877 which started on Long Wharf and spread south and east along that same street under gale force winds. It consumed businesses and homes, many of which had been lost to another horrific fire thirty-two years before. Typically persistent, the property owners cleared the destruction and built again in the heart of the village.

From Sag Harbor's founding in the early eighteenth century neighbors, friends, and families were personally connected, seeing each other daily, as they left for work, hung out the wash in the back yard, or walked to school. Most people knew—or knew of—everyone else, mainly because they went everywhere on foot. There wasn't much that escaped the local eyes and ears, and despite strong personalities and forthright scraps, the common understanding was to be civil to one another. The front porches became summer living rooms and most local gossip and the latest news were related by people going by. Gathering points within the neighborhoods, the churches and temple, the factories, the schools, the fire department, and the post office and dump brought people together, face to face. Nearly every neighborhood had its own shop or store within walking distance, usually a small grocery business that carried daily necessities and became the hub for the neighborhood. This helped cement the relationships between neighbors and provided the chance encounters that keep daily life interesting.

Sag Harbor's neighborhoods grew out from Main Street in random patterns. The early investors, provisioners, and whale ship owners lived in simple Federal houses at the southern end of Main Street, sometimes referred to as Captain's Row. As their owners prospered these little houses, many facing south or sideways, were added onto or consumed by larger, more lavish buildings in the latest style. At the same time, many modest antique "half houses" remained on small lots tucked between the big ones.

Oh, That's Another Story

By the 1890s the directors and executives of the Fahys Watch Case Factory built large homes on High Street, overlooking the factory. European immigrants, among them Jews who were experienced engravers and jewelers, were hired by Joseph Fahys when they arrived at Ellis Island. Fahys built simple gabled end houses for the workers, some on undeveloped lots east and south of the village center. The 1916 county map of Sag Harbor shows eight small houses labeled as Fahys Watch Case Co.

Italians lived above their stores in the business district, in a boarding house behind Main Street, and still later on Oakland Avenue. When we talked to Gabe and Diane Schiavoni, Gabe told us that Marty Trunzo would know—he lived over his barber shop. The Mazzeos, Ficorellis, and Berardis all settled on Oakland. But Diane, whose maiden name was Pintavalle, grew up on Hampton Street, two houses down from Yardley & Pino Funeral Home. "We had to be quiet out of respect for the funeral home." Diane added, "there is no class distinction here." Gabe continued, "you know, we all look out for one another. Like I tell everybody, the fisherman would trade two chickens for a bushel of clams. What our family used to do, they would go to the bank to try to get money and the banks wouldn't lend them, the Italians, any money. The only people who would loan us money were the Jews; just individual loans for almost nothing."

Several Polish families settled the area called Goat Alley at Henry and Division Streets. There were Zelinskis and Zaykowskis. Mrs. Daniels still spoke Polish in the 1970s and John Flak, our neighbor, would stop by to practice his childhood language. Little Dublin was on lower Main Street near Mashashimuet Park. Mrs. O'Connell had a beautiful old house on Main Street across from Otter Pond. Mrs. McLane spent her last years in a house next to the park. Eastville on the road to East Hampton was the home of Europeans, African- and Native Americans, many of whom were sailors and harpooners who shipped out on long whaling voyages. The late John A. Ward, former mayor, remembered that before World War II there was still competition among the kids, "Every nationality had its own territory. When I went to school I couldn't go in a separate territory alone. They'd beat you up like in New York!"

It has always been hard to discern which are the "better" neighborhoods of Sag Harbor. In the 1940s, '50s and '60s, still hard times, large properties were subdivided and affordable capes or ranch houses were built in the shadows of Main Street's mansions. The mix of rich and not-so-rich exists today but the character of many neighborhoods is being altered, again due to the influx of great fortunes. Mid-twentieth-century houses on tiny lots are being torn down and replaced by larger buildings. Tall privet hedges, *de rigueur* on Southampton estates, are being planted on Sag Harbor's single-lane streets and even more imposing gates are eliminating even a peek at the houses and gardens. John Ward commented, "Now they put bushes around…you know why it is? Air conditioning!"

Eastville is a half-moon shaped neighborhood of small houses on a few narrow streets east of the village center. Since the whaling days of the early nineteenth century free blacks and native Americans have made this area their home. Many were sailors expert at climbing ships' high rigging and were valued as skilled harpooners. Eastville is said to have been part of the underground railroad, a route for

Neighborhoods

Eastville's Heritage House

escaping slaves trying to reach Canada before the Civil War and emancipation in 1863. By the mid-twentieth-century the descendants and friends of the early families found the opportunity to buy undeveloped property and to build houses just east of Eastville. In all they created five private communities that provided summer homes to dozens of families from the New York and New Jersey metropolitan areas.

In 1981 Kathy Tucker, Elizabeth Bowser, Edith Jones, and others founded The Eastville Community Historical Society. Their unifying theme, Linking Three Cultures, emphasized the importance of all who lived so close together: African-Americans, Europeans, Montaukett and Shinnecock Indians. Their first project was driven by concern for the preservation of St. David AME Zion Church and Cemetery, and establishing the Eastville Historic District. In time, the new organization included the whole Eastville area and focused on the landmarking of significant buildings and finding a permanent office in which to store historic documents, photographs, and other materials. JoAnne Williams Carter, a later president of the historical society, said that there just wasn't enough space in St. David Church for the growing historical society and they were looking for another building.

Oh, That's Another Story

The Eastville Community Historical Society established their headquarters in 1996 in the Sears–Roebuck mail order house, shown here during a show of handmade quilts. The building arrived as bundles of pre-cut pieces delivered by train to Sag Harbor in 1925. Sears then sent a crew to assemble it. The distinctive Bungalow Style became the image of the ideal, affordable house for the American middle class. Once the house was restored and opened to the public as a museum and exhibition space, the members held a summer fundraiser, the annual Fish Fry, in the side yard. Coleslaw, corn bread, fried fish, cake, and lemonade were served on tables under shade trees. It is the major event of the year when everyone, black, colored, white, or "whatever you want to call yourself" can sit down and get to know each other. Russ Eberhardt was quite clear when he said, "I use the term colored because the word black doesn't really truly identify all of the people because many of us are mixed."

In 2013 I ran into Elizabeth Bowser at Schiavoni's Market and asked her how she was. She answered with a smile that she was 94 years old. Her grandmother, Carrie Smiley, was brought to Sag Harbor in the 1880s to be the seamstress for the wife of a whaling captain. Carrie was from Florida, born the slave daughter of a Native American woman and her plantation owner. She wasn't in Sag Harbor long before her childhood sweetheart arrived from Florida, they married and moved to Brooklyn. His name was T. Thomas Fortune, a printer who was hired to write for the Herald Tribune and went on to publish his own newspaper. Still close to her friends in Eastville, Carrie and her children came to Sag Harbor every summer, a pattern that was continued by Liz's parents when Liz and her brother were children.

Bob Maeder is from a Swiss family. He grew up in Eastville in the 1930s and lived in the old Cuffee house. The Cuffees and the Perdues, nearby neighbors, descended from the founders of the AME Zion Church 150 years ago. Their family names grace the headstones in the graveyard across from the church. Bob remembered the fun and freedom for neighborhood kids in the 1930s in a tape he recorded for the Eastville Community Historical Society in 1994.

"Up on the corner, that yellow house all fallen apart now, was I forget her name now," [Mrs. Johnson, then the resident of the historical society's house from Sears.] "She always had a parrot there and the parrot used to holler at us on our way to school." Bob cut almost a straight line from his house to school at Pierson. "We walked across the back lot, through Mrs. Perdue's back yard. Nobody seemed to mind if you walked through your yard in those days." Bob continued, "A wonderful lady, Mrs. Perdue. Her property abutted ours at the back. She always had a huge garden. Her and my mother used to swap vegetables — she gave us more than we gave her 'cause she had a great big garden and couldn't possibly eat all the stuff she grew." He also remembers the Pharaohs who lived on the corner near his house. They were the descendants of the Montaukett tribal leaders. "A really nice family. I used to hang around with Freddy, Billy, and Sammy. Mrs. P was very nice. She always invited us in for cookies. Then the old man Sam, Mr. P, a great big guy. Right behind him lived Charlie Butler who looked really like an Indian, almost like the guy on the nickel, had a pigtail in the back. He always raised rabbits. I have a good picture of him with a rabbit in his hand. We had wonderful neighbors in those days. We never had any trouble with neighbors in that area."

Neighborhoods

William Pickens, III told us about his Aunt Nan—Anna Cora Hawley—who lived next door to Bob Maeder. When he first came out here from Brooklyn instead of going to camp, Bill stayed with Aunt Nan as a child, "Aunt Nan's house had an outhouse.... I certainly wasn't used to that. She made sure I went out there early in the morning and cleaned everything... a great experience for me but a bit unsettling when I was ten.... I knew Bob, his mother, and made friends. I had Montauk Indian friends. They lived right down at the corner, Georgie Pharaoh.... Jim McMahon was a carpenter who lived down the block. He did work for my mother... In a world of segregation, discrimination, and hatred, we all got along out here."

Bill Pickens's family tree is vast and highlighted by letters and stories of both slaves, freed blacks, English, French, and Native Americans dating back three centuries. On his mother's side, a son of slaves from Guinea, West Africa was freed in 1715. He is also a direct descendant of the first mayor of Philadelphia, Humphrey Morrey whose term began in 1691. The mayor was a Quaker and when he died he freed all the family slaves, including his son's children by his mistress, a household servant. It is a fascinating and long story that Bill is researching through his collection of family documents with both a book in mind and a safe repository for the documents in a museum or at Yale, his grandfather's alma mater.

In the 1940s and 50s, family and friends of earlier residents began coming to Eastville from New York, New Jersey, and beyond to spend the summer. The five vacation communities established along the shore and in the wooded hills were called Azurest, Sag Harbor Hills, Ninevah, Chatfield's Hill, and Hillcrest Terrace. Michael Butler and his twin brother Martin have spent their summers in Sag Harbor since they were children. Michael's great-uncle, Jimmy Harris, arrived in the 1930s aboard his yacht and purchased a house on Division Street. In time, he acquired several cottages on Hampton Street in Eastville and rented them to friends while their summer homes were under construction.

Mr. Harris was a dean and department chairman of history and economics at Brooklyn Technical High School. Through his family connections, other professional African Americans, lawyers, doctors, teachers, and entrepreneurs learned of this "paradise by the bay." Families also stopped at Ivy Cottage, a little house on Hampton Street, for a room and a home-cooked meal. The building boom in the new vacation communities came at a time when many of Sag Harbor's Main Street stores were still empty with for-rent signs in the windows. Local contractors and tradesmen were more than happy with the increased business and got to know their new clients, their families, and friends.

Through the 1960s hundreds of summer people passed through Eastville. Many became full time residents and retired here. Now some of the children and grandchildren of the original African Americans have moved elsewhere and the six communities are evolving. Young, white, year round families are moving into the quiet streets.

By the end of the twentieth century few remembered how Goat Alley got its name or where it was. Seeing no signs of goats today I called a friend, Sharon York, who grew up there to find out more. She

Oh, That's Another Story

Spring on Atlantic Avenue

said her childhood home backed up against Frank Krupinski's house on Atlantic Avenue and that he had a butcher shop through a side door in his home. Across the narrow street next to Temple Adas Israel and near the elegant Academy of the Sacred Heart of Mary, Mr. Krupinski kept chickens, geese, and goats—hence the name.

In 1932, Mr. Krupinski built this hipped-roof house on the property across the street for his daughter and her husband, Dering Sleight. Originally, there were two front entrances. The one on the right led to a porch that Mrs. Sleight later closed in and used as a beauty parlor, one of several in private residences throughout Sag Harbor. Peter Hallock, a hair stylist, bought this house in the early 1980s, but had his salon in an outbuilding in someone else's backyard a few blocks away. A descendant of one of the earliest East End families, Peter was tall, astonishingly handsome, hilarious fun, and gave great hair cuts.

The mention of Mr. Krupinski brings up an interesting glitch when researching old street maps: family names were often spelled differently to make the pronunciation clearer or were misspelled in a mistake by the mapmaker. On a 1916 map in local historian Joseph Markowski's collection of old

Neighborhoods

The Bottle House

Oh, That's Another Story

documents the Krupinski's house is labeled "F. Gropenske." The house next door belonged to Sharon York's Lithuanian relatives known as the Bumleys. On the map it is labeled "Pumpeley." Joe pointed out that his grandfather's house is labeled "Makloskie," sort of a Scots version of his Polish name.

Legend has it that another house in Goat Alley was the home of Hannah Cook, a gregarious, outgoing lady who may have practiced one of the oldest professions. Part of this tale summons up the image of Hannah leaning out an upstairs window calling down to passers-by, "Come in, boys, only two are waiting." It is also reported that a local expression must have evolved from her carefree nature, "I don't care a Hannah Cook." Whether fact or fiction no one would or could tell. In fact, any question into serious calamity or illegal behavior, and especially the mention of brothels, has been met with the same answer, "Oh, that's another story," the local version of "off the record." That there were brothels in the village is undeniable in a port town, but the only ones we could talk about existed fifty years or more before our interviewees were born. One was located near the railroad platform just beyond the junction of Brick Kiln Road and Main Street but no one remembered it.

Not far from Goat Alley was the Bottle House, the home of the late Ida Abelman. An artist, Ida came to Sag Harbor from Brooklyn when many of her artist friends were settling in Springs, a rural area further east on Long Island. We will hear more about Ida and the years her family lived in Mashashimuet Park, but here we have an example of an old house becoming a local icon in the neighborhood for a very simple reason.

As a young boy Ida's son Fred used to dig up old bottles as a hobby. "My mother loved glass. Most are not really old, or antique. Some of them had notes attached like the Winter Blizzard of 1971, Dinner with Hans and Barbara." She set up shelves in the windows of her glassed-in front porch and arranged Fred's bottle collection where they would best catch the sunlight. "Someone threw a golf ball through the window," continued Fred. "I found out who did it but that's another name I won't mention. He apologized to me. This is the beauty of the village."

Several of the bottles with colored water in them froze and broke and the shelves were falling apart. Margaret Bromberg, Fred's sister, added, "We took them down. Shortly after our mother died," Fred interjects, "I was feeling a bit melancholy and decided to rebuild the shelves and the put bottles back up. As I am doing this, traffic begins to build up. People stopping and saying, 'Oh, the bottles are back!'" In 2014 the fabled porch was removed and the house moved sideways on the lot. The two ancient Linden dooryard trees were allowed to stand, sentinels from the past.

2

Religions

During the Great Depression children at St. Andrew Catholic school were told not to talk to kids from the Old Whalers' Presbyterian Church, just around the corner. John A. Ward told us when that started to change. "After the war all the priests—we've got one of every religion here—they all got together in the Whalers' Church. I remember the village went, the mayor, deputy mayor. We all went there to decide we all gotta shake hands and get together. That started the whole thing. It was a big thing at the time."

Even before the war, the Catholic priest had reconciliation in mind between the nationalities that attended Saint Andrew Church. Larry Burns heard this story from his parents. "My mother was Italian and my father Irish. They got married, they had a big reception hall, all the Italians over there and the Irish over here. The Italians thought they were better than the Irish and the Irish thought they were better than the Italians, and they never talked. The priest came in and said, 'Now look here. I'm going to stop this right now. We're going to all mix up and eat together. We're going to be family.'"

Oh, That's Another Story

Old Whalers' Church

Religions

The early Sag Harbor families were Presbyterians, Episcopalians, and Methodists. Roman Catholics in the mid-nineteenth century were mostly Irish immigrants, followed by Italians and Polish. Jewish jewelers from Poland, Russia, and Hungary agreed to come and work for the new watchcase factory in 1881 if they could have their own place of worship. They organized in 1883 and built their synagogue, then called Temple Mishkan Israel, in 1898. Two Baptist churches from the nineteenth century in the same neighborhood were converted to private homes.

The religious structures surviving today were all built in the mid- to late 1800s only a block or two away from each other. Considering that most people walked to church or had to groom, harness a horse, and hitch it to a carriage, it is easy to understand why the churches and the temple are located in the center of the village. Dirt roads combined with rainy nor'easters made for heavy going until the streets turned to ice and sleighs could be used.

The Presbyterian Church, known locally as the Old Whalers' Church, dates to 1844 and was designed by renowned architect Minard Lafever. Up until the hurricane of 1938 it had the most ornate steeple, a many tiered white wedding cake 187 feet high at its tip. During the storm, the steeple was torn loose from its moorings and fell sideways across the Old Burial Ground below. Still financially crippled by the Great Depression, the community cleared away the ornate pieces, with little hope of ever putting the steeple back up.

Dorothy Sherry, who taught poetry, recalled the tale of the poet, George Sterling, who lived in Sag Harbor as a child but left for San Francisco in the 1880s to work in real estate with his uncle Frank C. Havens (whose mansion still stands in Sag Harbor, now Cormaria Retreat House). Sterling went on to become California's unofficial poet laureate and "King of Bohemia," a leading character in the artistic circles of the Bay area. According to Dorothy, "Sterling had to leave Sag Harbor because he put a flag with a scull and crossbones on the top of the Whalers' Church steeple. Because of this naughtiness he was sent out to a school in Maryland." Not only is this Jolly Roger image a warning of poison or danger, when flown on pirate ships it was a signal that they intended to attack. This was not a welcome message from the Old Whalers' Church, then an important landmark for seafaring ships trying to find our harbor.

The Roman Catholic Church came to Sag Harbor in the early 1800s when Irish immigrants arrived seeking work in the households of well-to-do families who had prospered from the whaling trade. We had heard that Catholics were not accepted in the early days and that their first services had to be held in secret. We know that a few families gathered for worship at the home of Father Edward Burke on Burke Street until they bought the building formerly used by the Methodists on Union Street.

In 1872, a new Catholic church was built with gothic-style stained-glass windows in the sanctuary. Facing Division Street, the new church was across from the Episcopal Church and down the street from the Presbyterians. When asked, Miles Anderson, local attorney and descendant of an old local family, said, "If there was any kind of divide in Sag Harbor it was probably a religious divide. The old families

Oh, That's Another Story

St. Andrew R. C. Church

The former Methodist Church

were Protestant for the most part. The families that immigrated here in the 1880s [to work for the factory] were mostly Roman Catholics. That was the cultural divide. The neighborhoods were pretty much mingled together."

For years, Tuesday was Bingo Night at the Catholic school, across the street from St. Andrew Church. The game was popular with all ages as a social gathering and the chance to win some cash, and lamented when the game was discontinued. A greater sadness was the closing of the school that opened in 1877 as St. Andrew, later renamed Stella Maris, after serving the village for 134 years.

The Methodist Church may have been second in stature to the Old Whalers' Church but, high on a hill, it was as important a navigational landmark to early Sag Harbor sailors. The Methodists had erected a small church on Union Street in 1811. By 1834 they needed a larger building and considered two sites, one at Church and Sage Streets and another—their final choice—at the crest of High Street. The view of the harbor must have been spectacular and the location the most prominent in the village.

However, in a short time this choice turned out to be unfortunate, up a hill that in those days of snow, ice, or mud, was frequently impassable. In 1863 the church was moved down from the hill to Madison Street, a few steps from Main Street. The massive structure had to be taken apart, piece by piece, and put back together again on the new site at considerable cost. In 1938 this church, too, lost its tower in the great hurricane of that year. By the end of the twentieth century the congregation found the expense of upkeep too difficult and decided to sell this building, moving to a new church just beyond the village boundary. This church, too, has been converted to a private home.

In November of 2012 the *Sag Harbor Express* reported that a local boy scout was organizing a project to restore the belltower on St. David AME (African Methodist Episcopal) Zion Church. When we interviewed Rocco Liccardi, antique shop owner, he told us about a day in the 1960s when he was riding his bike and noticed that the church looked abandoned; the door was open. "I went up there on this ladder, all shaky. A black man came by and said, 'What are you doing?' I said, trying to be funny or something, 'I'm stealing the bell.'" The man explained that he was Kenneth Nelson and was the church's pastor. They became friends and later Rocco told him, "I am still so angry the church looks so bad. It needs to be painted. I will help you raise money. My mother and I will give a dinner. We'll send out invitations saying 'Indian Costume Optional' but you have to get Princess Nowedonah to be here so lots of people will come.' Eva Latch waited at the front gate with a cigar box for the money. People came and we started serving the food but where was the Princess? A big yellow taxi pulls up and there is this beautiful little woman all dressed in white buckskin. We think this is the Princess. She says to my mother, 'Mrs. Liccardi, it's Linda Gould from Mineola!'" The Princess never came, they made lots of money and the church was painted.

St. David AME Zion Church was organized in 1840 by Lewis Cuffee, a descendant of African Americans and local Shinnecock Indians, Charles Plato, and William Prime. The Methodist Episcopal Church had become crowded and a group of worshippers decided to buy land for a new church on Eastville Avenue. David Hempstead was on their building committee.

Dorothy Zaykowski in her history of Sag Harbor writes, "David Hempstead was accepted, a man admired and respected in the village by both black and white residents alike. It was his kindness, generosity, and, most of all his great faith that made him an outstanding leader in the black community." Mrs. Zaykowski goes on to quote Henry P. Hedges, historian, in a talk before the Sag Harbor Historical Society in 1896, "Who can deny that God made this man his witness in the African Church."

In the 1890s a set of Tiffany stained-glass windows was purchased from Sag Harbor's Christ Church Episcopal, which was undergoing renovation. Several groups raised money to acquire the windows for St. David: the Ladies Village Improvement Society, the Associated Sisters, and the Sunday School. Since 2000 the little church has been rented by the Methodists while their new church was being built, and then by the Triune Baptists.

Religions

St. David AME Zion Church

When Joseph Fahys moved his watchcase factory to Sag Harbor in the 1880s he brought Jewish workers from his New Jersey plant and hired more European immigrants arriving through Ellis Island. By 1900 the newcomers established an Orthodox synagogue called Temple Mishkan Israel and created a cemetery at the eastern edge of the Sag Harbor village. Margaret Bromberg explained that the temple was sited in a central location, at the core of a neighborhood. "The expectation for Orthodox Jews was that you walked to synagogue. You were not supposed to use your car on holy days."

Another congregation, predominantly Hungarian, organized and held services in the Engravers' Hall on Main Street. In 1918 the temple was in need of financial help and the two groups united and renamed the temple Adas Israel, now the oldest synagogue in Suffolk County. The Jewish cemetery at the outskirts of town remains divided with a simple fence separating Hungarians from Polish and Russians. My neighbor, Joe Markowski, related this story long ago. He was working in the temple basement when he noticed a change in the sound as he crossed the floor. It turned out that the original mikvah, an Orthodox ritual bath, had been boarded over and hidden beneath the floor for more than thirty years.

Temple Adas Israel

Religions

Christ Church, Episcopal

Oh, That's Another Story

The history of the Episcopal church in Sag Harbor began in 1845 with a small gathering at the old Arsenal on Union Street. For the next year they met in the former Presbyterian Church, then being used as a village hall, and purchased it in 1846.

The current Episcopal Church was built in 1884 and 1885 on the corner of Union and Hampton, catty-corner to St. Andrews Church. Designed in the then popular Gothic style, the church was painted in somber colors and topped with a slate roof. Mr. and Mrs. James Herman Aldrich, summer residents of North Haven, were active parishioners and donated many of the interior details including a marble alter and baptismal font, and a bronze lectern. A few years later Mrs. Russell Sage, another noted philanthropist in Sag Harbor, donated a new bronze bell. In 1912 Mr. Aldrich suggested adding a parish house behind the Church on Union Street. Mrs. Aldrich continued to support the church in 1914 by donating funds to build the rectory next to the church on Hampton Street.

Residents of the Eastville community make up a good part of the congregation attending Christ Church today. "It is a wonderful conglomeration of people at Christ Church," said JoAnne Williams Carter when we talked to her. "That's what I like about Sag Harbor." JoAnne continued that there was another reason she was drawn to Christ Church. "My mother was a Yemassee Indian from South Carolina…. My Indian name is Loves Eagles. This is why I started going to Christ Church, because of the eagle in the front of the church. I thought it was a sign that I should go there and I still think so."

The late Neal Hartman was in charge of flowers for the altar, contributed cookies to coffee hour, and whipped up comfort food for the sick. Any chore was an occasion for fun. Neal was also the regular bell ringer. Shortly after his death, the wood mounting for the bell was found to need repair. Parishioners and friends raised the funds to have it restored in his memory.

3

Industry

From the early days of the eighteenth century, industry was essential to the success of Sag Harbor. Sagaponack's farmers needed a deep water port to deliver their produce to America's colonial cities. Early shipping and whaling were supported by shipbuilders, sailmakers, coopers, blacksmiths, and rope works situated along the shore. In the 1850s, as whaling declined due to competition from kerosene and the discovery of petroleum, larger factories and, eventually, the production line became central to the working life of Sag Harbor.

Sag Harbor village is surrounded on three sides by water. Its Main Street enters the village from the south, runs straight north through the business district and out onto a long wharf extending into the harbor. By the year 2000 the brick factory buildings on Long Wharf housed a waterfront restaurant, a gym, a salon and spa, several shops, and the fabled Bay Street Theatre. Exotic yachts from all over the world flank the wharf, with the view beyond of graceful sailboats resting on their moorings. The harbor today is almost as crowded as it was when a forest of tall masts fenced the sides of the wharf and men hustled heavy loads into or out of ships' holds. In early Sag Harbor carts and horse-drawn wagons

Oh, That's Another Story

Long Wharf

jostled for access. Later, the railroad took over much of the shipping, its tracks curving onto the wharf so freight cars could sidle up to the big steam boats, loading passengers and freight for the trip to New England, New York City and beyond.

Prior to World War I, E. W. Bliss, a company in Brooklyn, N.Y. that manufactured torpedoes, maintained a workshop on the wharf and tested torpedoes in the bay. During World War II both Agawam Aircraft and Grumman Aircraft had factories in the old brick buildings. Grumman was still there in the 1960s, supplying parts for the Apollo lunar lander that went to the moon. By then, there was little traffic by sea, the steamers that carried passengers to Greenport, New York City, and New England had been scuttled. Rowboats were pulled up on the shore and a few sailboats rode at anchor within the breakwater.

As the factories closed the largest brick buildings grew hollow: no light shown from within and the walls were taken over by leafy vines, or as one old man once said to me, "those walls are covered in ivory." I'm sure he meant ivy. The wharf, a shrunken version of its former length, fell into disrepair. Fred Abelman remembers, "If there is anything that makes me believe in the spirit world it is that I sense in

Industry

Bulova Factory

Oh, That's Another Story

Sag Harbor remnants of the whaling era. I really felt as a kid that there were ghosts here and I was fascinated by it. The Long Wharf was totally ramshackle—you had to climb over broken pilings to get out to the end. The very base of it was completely ruined. I was always told by our mother you don't go out to the end of Long Wharf and, of course, we all were out on the end of Long Wharf. It was an example of how broken this village was…. I also think the fact that Montauk Highway (the main East–West route) didn't run through town—it was not on a main artery—made a big difference."

Fahys Watch Case Factory opened in 1882 and was by far the largest building in the village. In a short time hundreds of people were employed there. Every day at noon they streamed out of the huge brick building, running home for lunch. Later on, at the sound of the 12 o'clock whistle, they swarmed the luncheonettes nearby. Until it was gutted by fire in 1925, Fahys's Alvin Silver Company added to the throng of workers on Main Street. The traffic was so dense that a traffic light was installed at Main and Washington Streets. During the Great Depression, the watchcase factory went out of business and the village trustees searched for a buyer. The Bulova Watch Company came to town in 1937. With so many skilled workers already established here, production resumed right away. Though it slowed down during and after World War II, the factory stayed in business until 1975.

Jack van Kovics lived in Connecticut during his early childhood. He remarked that, "When the family came back here in 1955, I moved from Bridgeport, a gritty factory city to Sag Harbor, a gritty factory town." His wife, Susan Field, worked at Bulova in the early 1970s after High School. "It was fun. I was in the production scheduling department. We had this big table and huge books that charted the next step in the process." They brought her the bezels, she would look them up and make sure each bezel went to the right watchcase. Because of the value of silver, gold, diamonds and other jewels, there was tight control of these materials.

Still referred to locally as Bulova, the factory was renamed Watchcase Sag Harbor, the old building rehabilitated into a rambling collection of luxury condominiums and new townhouses with all the amenities. First proposed in 1981, when the factory was sold, it has taken more than thirty years to near completion. When we asked about Bulova it seemed as if almost everyone had worked there. Barbara Fiore, who runs an upholstery and drapery business, remembered her job, "They would bring the precious stones in gelatin capsules. We set tiny diamonds in the prongs and folded the prongs down. We had to count the diamonds in each capsule as we set them." The floors were swept every night. They even saved the gold shavings from the emery boards used to smooth the metal watchcases.

Bill Pickens's older brother worked at Bulova in the summer while he was at Lafayette College. He worried about the pollution he saw. His mother made sure he washed carefully when he got home. Craig Rhodes, architect, had a summer job at Bulova while attending Pratt Institute. "Benny Menaik was the fastest worker. He sat across from me. He was always the first in line to punch the time-clock at the end of the day, too. See this bump on my thumb? That's from working at Bulova. We took the ladies' watchcases and shaved down the interior edge so the movements fit exactly. We used a tool with several

Fahys Watch Case Company ca. 1880s

points and my thumb developed a really big callous. Back at school I was using a sharp blade and sliced through that callous, it got infected, and I ended up in the hospital."

Bulova's huge buildings towered over the village houses and its large windows offered good views of their back yards. One of our favorite interviews was in 2011 with May Kelman, then 97, a Main Street resident now a hundred years old. Her husband, Dr. Irving Kelman, came to Sag Harbor in 1948 and took over the dental practice of a Dr. Gordon who had been declared an "essential" during the war when everyone else had been called to duty. "Sag Harbor needed a dentist and Dr. Gordon made a fortune. We bought the house at 125 Main Street and, when Irving started his practice, he left Dr. Gordon's sign in the window. Dr. Holmberg [a revered local physician] said, 'You know what Doc? Do yourself a favor. Take that sign out of the window. Everybody hated that bastard.'" I hope Dr. Gordon's descendants don't read this. I doubt they will as May Kelman went on to say, "Mrs. Gordon hated Sag Harbor. She had two wardrobes, one for Sag Harbor and another for when she went away." She couldn't wait to get out of town.

Oh, That's Another Story

The Kelmans' old Main Street house was an antique, perched up on a bit of lawn above the current sidewalk and the backyard stretched to Church Street and the high brick walls of the Bulova factory. "One day when I had lots of laundry on the clothes line it started to rain. I ran out to get the laundry and from the factory windows were all these people calling out 'Hurry up!'" The garage in that backyard had a basketball hoop and lots of kids stopped to play on their way home from school. "The mothers knew where to pick up their kids."

Other factories were built closer to the southern boundary of the village, almost "out of town." The small factory building on Jermain Avenue near Oakland Cemetery goes back almost one hundred years to 1918 when the block structure was built by William S. Eaton. The head engraver for Fahys Watch Case Company in the 1880s, he later founded Eaton's Engravers and Printers Machinery Company and was noted for his invention and manufacture of a rotary photogravure device. Mr. Eaton went on to hold many patents for engraving and related machinery. During our interview with Miles Anderson, local attorney, he surprised us by pulling a small object out of a file drawer. "That's what they made," he said, "See the little X?" Cross hairs. "It's a gun site, from Eaton." Miles had picked it up as a teenager on a school tour of the factory in 1955. For many years this factory was the home of Schiavoni's Plumbing and Heating.

According to David Lee in *Voices of Sag Harbor* and former vice president of the company, "Rowe Industries was first where an Italian restaurant is now; then they built the plant on the turnpike." It was reported in the *Express* on February 7, 1963 that:

> The Sag Harbor plant of Rowe Industries, Inc., manufacturer of small motors for some of the nation's most important firms, was completely gutted by fire last night. Robert Rowe, head of the company estimated the damage at more than $1 million. Rowe Industries employs between two and three hundred people and its payroll is $16 to $22 thousand a week.

After the fire the firm moved twice again and finally was bought by Sag Harbor Industries which still operates at the old Rowe site on the Turnpike south of the village border. Sag Harbor Industries was started in the late 1940s by Charles Edison, Governor of New Jersey and son of Thomas A. Edison. He summered in the Hannibal French house on Main Street and became very involved with saving the old Custom House from demolition. Today the Custom House is sited on land donated by Edison.

For many years a huge Hortonsphere, used for the storage of natural gas, was affectionately known as "the blue ball." It was tucked down behind the Main Street stores on a site that had a history of oil and gas production and storage. This structure is one of only two which Whitney painted that is no longer standing. The other is the Academy of the Sacred Heart, once on the site of the elementary school.

At the height of whaling in the mid-nineteenth century there was a spermaceti factory on the site of the blue ball for refining whale oil, the best for making candles. After the demise of whaling in the 1850s

Industry

Hortonsphere

it became a gas works, where charcoal was processed to produce gas. Still later it was purchased by the electric company which distributed natural gas and erected the blue ball as a holding tank for excess gas in the system.

In the 1950s, John Ward built a garage for auto repair near this site. After the hurricane of '38 took out the Whalers' Church steeple and the Methodist steeple the blue ball served as a major landmark for sailors. Sometime in the 1970s an old underground tank was found, full of oil. Barbara Fiore remembered that a sample sent for testing was reported to be whale oil, over 100 years old. Before the Long Island Lighting Company decided to tear down the blue ball, many people thought it should have a fancy paint job to look like a big basketball, or the earth viewed from space, or a huge aquarium with fish and whales swimming in it. The blue ball was torn down in 2006 and is still missed.

4

Farms

John Cilli and his wife Anita were our first interviewees, before we were sure where this book would lead us. It was the best beginning. John's memories are a clear picture of farming's vital contribution to the life of the village, through the Great Depression, during the slow loss of factory jobs, to the return of prosperity.

Cilli's farm or Cove Side Dairy was founded in 1922 by John's father, Vitali, fourteen years after arriving from Italy. It was the last farm to process milk and have cows in Sag Harbor Village. The Cilli brothers delivered bottled milk to Sag Harbor, North Haven, and Noyac and gave out bonus sticks of Juicy Fruit gum to the kids. If you weren't home John and Dominic had the keys to your house and would put the glass bottles in your refrigerator. Most houses were never locked anyway.

The herd numbered sixty-five at its height and stopped traffic on Glover Street going from the barn to pasture twice a day. Sometimes gentle but persistent cows would find a hole in the fence and take a walk. One was found asleep at Baron's Cove Inn. Gabe Schiavoni said, "We used to wake up and find them in our yard [on Bayview Avenue]." His wife Diane added, "It would be fun to see them in the spring. They would gallop out of the barn." When a whole bunch ambled out onto the Redwood peninsula, John pursued them in his truck with the ahoogah horn. As he drove the winding streets blowing the horn the cows slowly followed him back home.

We see John often, driving by in his truck, the back filled with mysterious treasures. Whitney recalled talking to him one day: "He noticed that my hands were rough, from all that turpentine and washing my paint brushes. John said. 'I have something for you.' He jumped out of the pickup and reached into the back for a jar of ointment. 'Here, rub this on your hands everyday.' I'm not sure what it was but it worked."

Early in the twentieth century, the family cow was still a familiar sight in Sag Harbor and there were several dairy farms. Another farm belonged to John Cilli's Uncle Anthony and was located in a large open field at the end of Montauk Avenue, on the other side of the village.

"My cousin, Milly Cilli" …
"*What*? we laughed."
"The first three were Milly, Willie, and Lily, the next, Helen, and then Tony," added John with a chuckle.

Leander C. Aldrich's farm was at the corner of Brick Kiln and Noyac Roads and the family owned a small butcher shop on Suffolk Street. In 1930, Aldrich advertised his Hardscrabble Farm in the *Express*:

"Pure Milk, Buttermilk, Heavy Cream sold and delivered."

Aldrich's descendant the late Olin Edwards told us, "They kept pigs and cows and delivered by horse and buggy." Just beyond their barn was another farm, Nolan's Head of Pond Dairy. Markowski's Dairy was on Harrison Street and the cows were taken down to Havens Beach to graze on marsh grass. John Ward told us there used to be an island in the harbor, called Gull Island (Dorothy Zaykowski's history recalls its Indian name, Mankesack Island, or Stony Island) and that you took the road near Cormaria to get there. John Ward said, "They used to take the cows out there, leave 'em, and bring them back a week or so later." Old glass milk bottles with the names of local dairies can sometimes be found in Sag Harbor antique shops and online.

There were chickens in backyards all over Sag Harbor up until the 1970s. John Ward remembered, "We had chickens, I raised pigeons. There was a big chicken farm back there beside the library. They had a little cart in there with the corn that they ran down the length of that building to feed the chickens. That was a big building…in back of all the houses on Main Street." Ann Yardley Hansen said, "Daddy had a chicken coop in back of the funeral parlor [their home on Hampton Street]." The small R & R Farm on Redwood still sells fresh eggs today at a self-serve stand. The money goes in a jar or box; exact change helps.

Farms

Cilli's Farm

Oh, That's Another Story

R & R Farms

In 2011 the Sag Harbor code was amended to allow chickens to be raised again—only six hens and no roosters. Crowing at dawn by weekend revelers is barely tolerated but roosters are not to be heard at all.

Since the 1990s, Bette Lacina and Dale Haubrich have produced enough organic vegetables to sell to restaurants as well as at Farmer's Markets and at their stand on the Sag Harbor Turnpike. They till, plant, and harvest their crops without the help of motorized equipment and tread lightly on the soil. They also sell eggs from free-range chickens which are rotated about the garden as the crops are harvested. The hens forage for insects and leftover greens, benefiting their eggs and the soil. Hoop houses extend the season for leafy greens to late fall and early spring. Bette and Dale's farm stand is self-help: bring your own bag and put your money in the little metal box.

Carol Olejnik's tomato stand has been a colorful and convenient feature on Main Street for over forty years. "It started with me giving my nephew something to do. That didn't last long and my mother took it over. When she got too old, I did it, and she sat on the porch. She'd talk to everyone and say those

Milk Bottles from three Sag Harbor Dairies

tomatoes aren't as good as they used to be!" Carol doesn't actually grow the tomatoes. At first she got them from a farmer in Bridgehampton, later from a woman in Southampton. A descendent of that family, Tim Kraszewski, raises them today. Carol added, "I enjoy talking to the customers. I don't know all their names but it is fun. Friends stop and chat, so it's not just a business, it's a social thing."

Oh, That's Another Story

Spring chickens

5

Shops and Businesses

Herman Klein's grocery store at Madison and Jermain was in the center of a residential neighborhood, a block from school and a favorite stop for kids. Here, painted from a 1941 photograph, the famous Moylan sisters, national radio singing stars, hang out with the boys. The littlest, chugging a soda, is Brad Hansen, whose family owned the 5 & 10-cent store on Main Street. Later H. Klein's became Johnny & Eddie's. In the late 1950s this is where Patricia and Eileen Archibald bought their daily cupcakes on the way to school at the Academy. "One day we went in and Johnny said, 'Here come the 'Cup-Cake Girls.' My sister said to me, 'We are not going back there. That was not a nice thing to say!' So we stayed away for two days." After that it was okay. Her parents knew Johnny and Eddie. Gabe Schiavoni referred to "Uncle Eddie, Uncle Eddie Rozzi." Asked if he was his real uncle he paused and replied, "The Rozzi's and the Schiavonis all intermarried in like two or three different ways."

Five clusters of markets developed on the major streets that radiate out from the center of downtown Sag Harbor and the wharf. Each group of stores was the focus of a neighborhood and there were tiny shops sprinkled between the neighborhood centers, usually in someone's home. The Great Depression

Oh, That's Another Story

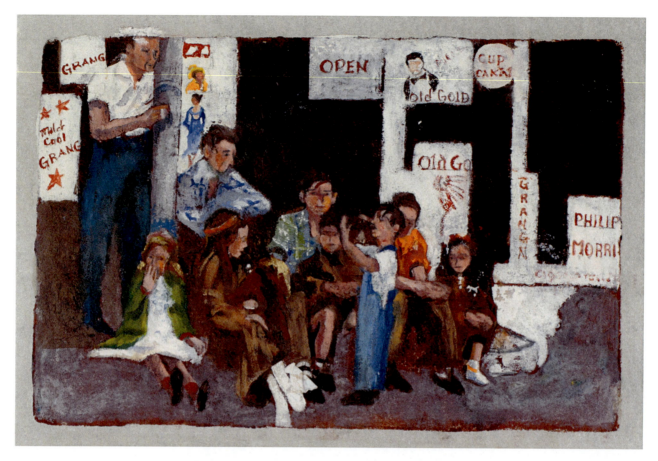

H. Klein's, later known as Johnny & Eddie's

hung on in the village and deprivation continued during World War II. Gas was rationed; if you had a car you rarely used it. Many women in Sag Harbor never drove. The husbands did the weekly marketing and the daily shopping was done on foot. Or you called the store, gave them your order and sent your children to fetch it for you. A grocery store would be close to a meat market, or the two might be combined. Most of these clusters were no more than two or three blocks from each other, so running to the store for a missing ingredient only took a few minutes. A family developed a route, stopping at one shop for a favorite item or just going there because the owner was a friend.

When we asked our interviewees, "Where did you shop?" the names were rattled off in no particular order: Korsak's Madison Market, Kulczycki's, Mahar's, Scholtz's, Cleveland's, Distefano's. As new owners took over, a store's name would change but the new name would take a while to sink in. People remember the names the stores had when they first went there, when they were kids, or when they first moved to Sag Harbor. Some businesses changed location and took their names with them. A store on the corner of Jermain Avenue and Hampton Street changed hands a few times between the 1930s and the 1970s, run by Mrs. Emmel, then in succession by Mahars and Joseph Parker. It was called Fields' when Barbara Fiore, her six-year-old daughter Mary Lee, and her baby sister lived nearby on Montauk Avenue. "I would call the grocery store, place an order, and watch Mary Lee go down the street to the store. She would pick up what we had ordered." Mary Lee added, "Sometimes the Stokes boys would escort me if the bag was too big."

The Korsaks came from Poland and opened their first store, a meat market, on Washington Street, near the watchcase factory. They then moved the market to the corner of Madison and Jermain and called it the Madison Meat Market. At the time, H. Klein & Son was across the street and on the other side of Madison was Roulston's, one of a small chain of Long Island grocers. Mr. and Mrs. Korsak, both noted butchers, then moved the Madison Meat Market to Division Street next to St. Andrew Church. Their daughter Ann continued to work in the store after she married Stanley Bubka but it was still thought of as Korsak's.

Michael Butler, who summered with his grandmother further down Division was a regular. "Korsak's made the best potato salad and the best baked beans I've ever tasted. Mrs. Korsak put something like baking powder or soda in the beans; you never had a reaction! And the potato salad was just wonderful!" The Madison Market sign is still there above the changing names on the windows. As I write, the Madison Market has a new name. What was called Agave is now Cilantro and is serving up Mexican fare.

Tony Kulczycki's on Hampton and Elizabeth Streets was a big favorite. (In case you want to say it, that Polish name sounds like "Kolcheski.") Diane Schiavoni was sent there by her mother on errands all the time. "It was fun to go to Kulczycki's. Tony was crazy, too. One day I went to get milk. He says 'What kind of milk do you want? Do you want this kind of milk?' he says, waving his hand across his face… 'past your eyes?'" (That's as in "pasteurized.")

If you were too busy to leave home, vendors would pass through the streets or come to your house on a regular basis. Bob Maeder, resident of Eastville in the 1930s, remembers them well. "Whiskey Big Bill Scarlato would come around with a real old truck, with his fish on the back of it. Nate Hildreth was the ice man, used to come with big chunks of ice. The kids used to chase after him; he'd always chisel off a piece of ice for the kids to suck on like a lollipop. He was a good guy, too. And Mr. Berkstein used to come around with his bakery truck. And I remember, I can still smell it, all that good stuff he had in the back there. And there was a guy, I think it was Mr. Matles, with a fruit wagon. He'd come around with apples and pears, and that kind of stuff." Margaret Abelman Bromberg remembered, "My father [Larry Abelman] got up at 3 in the morning, drove to Washington Market in the city. He trucked potatoes and eggs into the city and then produce out. It was a Jewish business."

Federico's Superette was a short walk on a sandy path on Henry Street from our first Sag Harbor home. Whitney Hansen lives along this path and now her grandchildren can pad their way down to the Harbor Market, the latest incarnation of this store, without crossing a street. The fire house, Murray Hill Hose Co., and Temple Adas Israel still stand a bit up the hill. The largest structure opposite the

Oh, That's Another Story

Federico's Superette

store, Goat Alley Gallery, was originally a hotel in Brooklyn. In 1910, the site is recorded as C. H. Vaughn's grocery store. Local lore has it that the three-story building was floated to the harbor on a barge and then hauled straight here from the wharf. Jim Federico recalled a conversation with Jim McMahon, longtime Mayor of the village: "I wish I had a recording every time I spoke with Jim McMahon. He told me he could remember when they brought that building here. He said 'I can still see it coming down Division Street.'"

Jim Federico mentions Lucia Haile, a lovely lady and an artist who lived nearby. "Lucia was in my store every day, as was Whitney Hansen! One day Lucia takes a cart and is going down the first aisle and in walks Walt Zaykowski [from his home down the block]. 'Oh, Walter, I've got to talk to you,' she says, 'I have a piano that has to be moved…. When can you do that?' 'I can do it right now,' he says, 'I'll go home and get Paul' [his eldest son]. Then she says, 'Jim, can I leave these things with you?' Sure. She had some perishable things so I put them in the fridge. About a half-hour later she comes back: 'Piano's moved. Now I can finish my shopping.' Walt had what is often called a junk yard, but it was full of good used and hard-to-find stuff. My husband and I were looking for twelve cast-iron radiators and found

Shops and Businesses

Emma Corwin's Yarn Shop

them all at Walt's. Once Jim Federico needed a ladder to get up on his tall building. 'Sure Fed, whatever you want Fed. Yeah Fed. Okay Fed. Yes Fed.'" At some point a newly arrived neighbor decided that Walt's yard was unsightly. A petition saying it had to be cleaned up was passed around. No one in the neighborhood would sign it.

In the 1950s Emma Corwin had a yarn store downtown on Main Street. Later she moved down the street from Federico's on Henry Street to this house, a Gothic Revival cottage surrounded by a porch and picket fence. You could see her skeins of yarn in all colors on the windowsill. It was a time when knitting was not just an economical necessity but a popular pastime, often accompanied by cups of tea and lots of talk. Whitney remembers walking by with her four-year-old daughter, "Miss Corwin tied pieces of yarn to her fingers, a different color for each one."

Hundreds of factory workers lived within the confines of this small village, before the days of commuting. They spent their earnings in the shops, stores, restaurants, banks, and hired local tradesmen. If anyone left the village to shop elsewhere it was probably a special occasion and the money was spent in another small town, similar to and not far from Sag Harbor. In the 1920s and '30s many families took the steamer from Long Wharf to Greenport to buy clothes for the school year. In the 1940s the rail spur to Sag Harbor was discontinued and the steamships had gone out of business. World War II and gas rationing made travel more expensive and less appealing. Most shopping was local.

Oh, That's Another Story

Sag Harbor's Main Street is still the heart of this village. Today its stores and shops enable people to leave their cars at home and walk. To be without a car today is a new life-style choice supported by alternative transportation, the county "blue bus," or the Hampton Jitney that goes to New York City and beyond. A couple of well known residents took the Hampton Jitney to business appointments in Manhattan and spent much of their creative time in the peace of the village. The late Lanford Wilson, playwright, was seen often heading on foot for the library or his favorite watering hole, The American Hotel. Gahan Wilson, cartoonist, dressed in a tan trenchcoat and, with a black briefcase in hand, took the Jitney once a week to make the rounds of the art departments of *The New Yorker, GQ,* and *Playboy* magazines.

A note on famous people in Sag Harbor: the old Sag Harbor attitude is to say hello as if they are normal people. When John Steinbeck lived here he went fishing with Bob Freidah, school administrator, and Bob Barry, owner of the hardware store. I remember hearing years ago that John Harrington, our police chief, visited Hurd Hatfield, star of the 1945 film Oscar Wilde's *The Picture of Dorian Gray*. Hurd had retired to Ireland and John while on vacation sought out his house there and was invited in for tea or a drink. Hurd was still in his pajamas. A little bit of Sag Harbor a long way from home.

The Sag Harbor Variety Store is legendary—everyone's favorite—and is the last of its kind on the East End. Still called the The Five and Ten Cent Store by locals, it has life-size cutouts of Jimmy Dean and Marilyn Monroe from the 1950s in its window. Out front, a coin operated bucking bronco and a fire engine complete with bell and siren are magnets for small children—proof that they can still be enthralled the way their grandparents were. That fire siren from that miniature truck always makes me check my rear view mirror for the real engine as I drive by.

Inside the Variety Store, the aisles are packed with thousands of small items. It is the go-to source for all household needs, sewing supplies, crafts, toys, socks, underwear, and sweatshirts with whales on them. You can find feathers, flowers, fabrics, and oil cloth. Over the years, among the odd-ball things on my own shopping list have been Easter baskets and cellophane grass to use as photo props in October and Christmas ornaments in July. No matter what the holiday, Phil Bucking would disappear into the basement and come up with just what I needed. Recently a last minute upholstery project required old-fashioned burlap webbing. They had it and the salesperson knew just where to find it.

The credit for the Variety Store's survival goes to the Bucking family, Roseann and her late husband, Philip H. Bucking Jr., who took it over in 1970. Today the Buckings' daughter, Lisa Field, carries on the tradition with continuing help from her mother. We talked to her brother Philip J. Bucking, who said the business "first began across the street near the current Wharf Shop in 1922. The Hansens moved it to this location and then my father bought it. Upstairs was once used for Village meetings. The ceilings were very high with a U. S. flag with forty-eight stars. The building dates back to the mid-1800s." Barbara Fiore recalled, "When Phil Jr. bought the Five and Ten, no one could understand why he left Bulova with all the benefits. Everyone at Bulova thought he was crazy. They have made a really good run of it." With his wife Diane, young Phil runs the Sag Harbor Garden Center in the old freight depot

Shops and Businesses

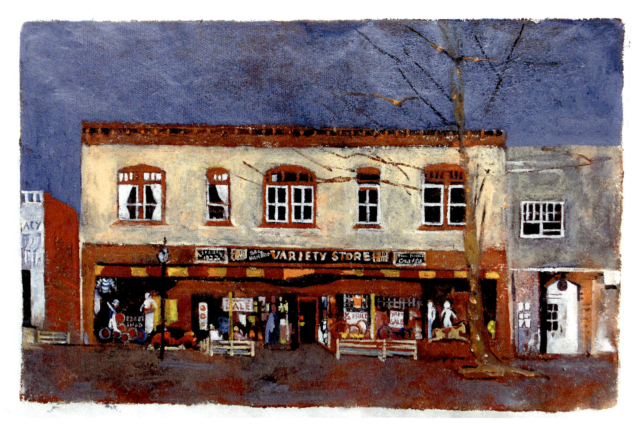

Sag Harbor Variety Store

which was moved up from West Water Street. On the walls are some of his collection of vintage photographs and memorabilia from the Long Island Railroad's Sag Harbor branch in his Sag Harbor Railroad Museum.

A store that has Jimmy Dean and Marilyn in the window is sure to attract celebrities. They need the basics too. Back in the late 1970s I had just put my purchases on the counter when Nancy Simonson, busy in real estate, came rushing into the store. "Paul Newman's coming up the block!" she exclaimed. In seconds he strode into the store, looking for a T-shirt. He came often in those days to the racetrack in Bridgehampton and was no stranger to Sag Harbor. At the cash register the elderly lady with curly white hair seemed to go into shock. I quickly handed her my exact change and said, "Don't worry. I'll leave so he'll come straight to you." "God bless you, dear," she said, with a huge smile.

In the 1920s Roulston's of Brooklyn, Long Island, and Staten Island was a chain of 700 small grocery stores. Sag Harbor's Roulston's was at the crossroads of Madison Street and Jermain, and later moved downtown to Main Street. Angelo Schiavoni worked there for twelve years learning the grocery business before moving down the street to his own place. Joe Markowski showed us a photograph of his father, Jocko, as a dashing young man in a starched collar, full white apron and a white cotton jacket,

Oh, That's Another Story

Roulston's Shopping List

standing in front of the Roulston's store after it had moved to Main Street. The sign in the window advertises whole wheat bread at 10 cents a loaf. In those days, orders could be placed by phone and home delivery made life easier. Joe also showed us Roulston's shopping list with the local phone number, Sag Harbor 3. Miles Anderson, local attorney, remembers Roulston's: "They were very old-fashioned. They put all the items you needed together and wrapped it up with plain paper."

The late John Ward was a former village trustee, mayor, Yacht Club commodore, mover and shaker of Sag Harbor. He was one of ten children and grew up on Bay Street. "We shopped on Main Street, at Roulston's and the A. & P. My father died young, so I had to go to work at thirteen years old. Every nickel I made had to go home and it helped a good deal. My oldest brother went and got married so I had to do all the chores, cut firewood. I had chickens and kept the vegetable garden. I raised pigeons. Mother was a very smart lady. She went shopping with a list of things to buy and had the price for each thing right on the list. When you went to the grocery store one of the clerks would put a broom against the counter and charge you for it. 'Oh, it ain't yours?' The clerk said don't fool with that girl; she knows what she's getting right down to the penny."

The Great Atlantic & Pacific Tea Company, founded in 1859, became a nationwide chain of grocery stores known as A & P. It became a popular store in downtown Sag Harbor. The Reverend and Mrs. North ran the Tuller School at Maycroft on North Haven and Mrs. North had a huge yellow retriever called Ricky. Barbara Fiore, the North's daughter-in-law, remembered Ricky going every day to the A & P to get a bone. "He sat at the side of Route 114 and waited for someone to pick him up and drop him

Shops and Businesses

Schiavoni's Market

off at the A & P. One day he got there at the same time as the bone man who was picking up the extra bones. The butcher had to lock him in the freezer so he wouldn't go for the bone man." After he got his bone, Ricky set out on a daily tour around the village. There were ladies who wouldn't plant flowers on his route. Completing his walk he would return to the foot of the bridge to North Haven and wait for someone to pick him up and take him home. "At the end of the day a strange car would drive up, the back door opened, and out would come Ricky."

"It was in 1941 when Gabe Schiavoni Sr. and his brother Vincent started a little grocery on Main Street," said Victoria Schiavoni. "Vincent was killed in a blackout drill. Because he was a fireman he ran across Main Street to the firehouse and was struck by a car…. When Vincent was killed, his brother Gabe did not want to continue with the store, he was just too distraught. So my father-in-law, Angelo, (another Schiavoni brother) bought the business from Gabe." Later, Angelo bought the Santacroce's building, the current location. For a while Rosalie Jacobs ran her children's clothing store called the Cracker Barrel in the space now stocked with fruits and vegetables.

Oh, That's Another Story

Victoria Schiavoni's late husband, Joe, worked in the store for his father, Angelo, from the time he was ten years old along with his brother John. "Joe would deliver items on his bike or walk, John did the same thing, and did that until the war was over." John and Joe took over the store in 1967 when Angelo retired. It continues in the same family, and is now run by Vicki's nephew Matt. A long time ago, Whitney Hansen, who has been shopping at Schiavoni's since the 1960s, lost her checkbook. A couple of years later her phone rang. "This is Joe Schiavoni. We are renovating the cash register area and we just found your checkbook under the old counter."

Sag Harbor's Main Street in the factory era provided for everyone's everyday needs and then some. The ads in the local newspapers hint at refinements available in local shops that we wish we had today. In the January 3, 1930 issue of the *Sag Harbor Express*, the public is encouraged:

> For Safety's Sake, Park Your Car in the Bay View Garage While Shopping or Attending the Movies. Reasonable Prices."

In addition to the essential shops, the banks, the markets, the drug stores, and insurance agencies, there was Osborne, Thompson and Gregory, a furniture store that also sold coffins. William M. Cook's department store carried ladies all-silk hose and woolen underhose. Another newspaper ad announced:

> Woodward Brothers' new crop of molasses just arrived from New Orleans—Bring your jugs and pails and get the real thing!

There were several tailors' shops that also did dry cleaning. The last dry cleaning establishment in Sag Harbor closed its doors in 2011. In the window was a collection of old flat irons, early electric irons, steam irons, and related antique tools of tailoring—a glimpse of Sag Harbor's continuing fascination with mechanical and electrical innovations.

When Patricia Archibald was twenty-one years old, she decided to open a beauty shop, Sagg Harbour Coiffures. By the 1970s, there were fewer vacant store fronts in the village and Suffolk Electric Motors was moving to the factory building on Jermain Avenue, leaving an empty shop next to the Corner Bar. She asked Stan Zlobec, who owned the building, if she could rent the space next to his dry cleaning business. He said, "You're a kid!" Patti is tall, pretty, and knew a thing or two about hair—a graduate of beauty school. No doubt, too, that she was direct and persuasive.

In Sag Harbor, there were and still are small beauty shops scattered through the neighborhoods in people's homes, their fame spread by the grapevine. The aforementioned salon of Peter Hallock during the 1980s was in a renovated garage on Palmer Terrace. Debbie Rossow worked from her house next to the Cove Deli on Main Street. Doris Gronlund, the famed owner of Sagalund clothing store, still goes to Frankie, a hairdresser who "is in a little house in the back on Bayview Avenue."

Marty's Barber Shop

Oh, That's Another Story

Sagg Harbour Coiffures

Before the 1960s it was almost unheard of to mix barbering with hairdressing, too embarrassing for women and too humiliating for men. The barbershop was the men's club of a working village, a place to relax and catch up on the latest news. Rocco Liccardi was sent as a child to get his hair cut at Vincent Alioto's on the second floor of a building near the movie theater. "He had the most incredible barbershop you've ever seen. The damned thing burned down! It was a crazy building with long windows and you went up these creepy steps. We used to love to go there." Rocco added that each seat was in a little fenced area, with a gate like a horse corral. "There was lots of cowboy stuff. We loved it."

Marty Trunzo retired from his barber shop in 2011 and, in his nineties, has a remarkable memory for people and places. He arrived from Italy at the age of eleven and before long was cutting hair in people's homes. "You couldn't get a job in 1932. I remember six to seven feet of snow piled up in the center of Main Street." While still young he apprenticed with Samuel Mazzeo, a barber on Madison Street.

In 1939 he opened his own shop on Main Street in a little building south of the library that had been a studio. Like so many Sag Harbor houses, this building later was moved to another site in Noyac. Marty continued to cut hair in part of what now is Schiavoni's market. In 1965 he had to find a new space. Mrs. Simon had just closed her clothing store and said, "Marty you can have my building." Marty was touched by her offer but told her he couldn't afford it. She said when you have the money, then you will pay me."The Jewish people are good-hearted people," he told me. As Marty said once to Fred Abelman, "You know, your people took good care of me." A note on Mrs. Simon's regard for money: Fred recalled that, to save electricity, she didn't turn the lights on in her store until a customer came in the door.

Other store owners were noted for their generosity and good faith. Vicki Schiavoni remembered Mr. Spitz's store when she and Joe first set up an apartment. They paid $25 as the downpayment and the rest over time for appliances and furniture.

In the early 1960s, while running his first antique business, Rocco Liccardi was persuaded by his landlady, Mildred Dickinson, to buy the building she had inherited from her father, Harry Youngs. Mr. Youngs repaired cars and bicycles and had a gas pump out front. Rocco, just starting out, said he couldn't afford to buy the building but Mildred said not to worry, "She said, 'Go to Mr. Gaines [at the bank] and ask him for the money. I've already called him and he's gonna wait for you.' So I went to see him. Mr. Gaines said, 'Now Rocco, what do you have for collateral?' So I said what does that mean? He said, 'Do you own anything?' No, I'm only twenty-two years old. I have an Italian Vespa and I have a black Afghan dog, from a very good kennel! I stood up very tall and I said to him, 'Mister Gaines, I am very young, I am very honest, and if I say I am going to pay, I will pay…and I will make that building as nice as I can and you will be proud of me. My father told me to ask you how much I have to pay a month. He said, 'It will cost you $68 a month.' $68 a month? I paid Harry Youngs $20 a month! 'Now wait a minute,' he says, 'you will own the building and you will get the rents.'" He explained to Rocco that he would have the $20 for his space, plus $20 from the barber, and $30 for the apartment upstairs for a total of $70, a $2 a month profit. "Gimme the pen, let me sign!"

In 2014 Rocco still owned the building.

In 1877 Addison Youngs sold his Bridgehampton farm and bought The American Hotel with his father-in-law and partner William Freeman. During the factory days in the 1930s, the hotel was the only place in town where traveling salesmen could have a good dinner, a bath, and a clean room for the night for $2.25. All meals were 25 cents and for 25 cents extra the meal would be brought to your room. Jack Youngs, a direct descendent of Addison Youngs, recalled, "Sometimes a drunk would sneak in through the back door, go upstairs and find a bed for a night." But on the whole it was a respectable place.

Jack Youngs visited his grandparents at the hotel in the early '50s and later lived there while he attended the local high school. The Youngs family would spend their evenings in the front parlor. He showed us photos of the family around the Christmas tree in what became a hotel dining room. "I had a scooter and rode through the rooms after dinner." Later, when he was a bit older, Jack lived on the third floor of the hotel. Asked how it was, he answered, "Scary!"

Oh, That's Another Story

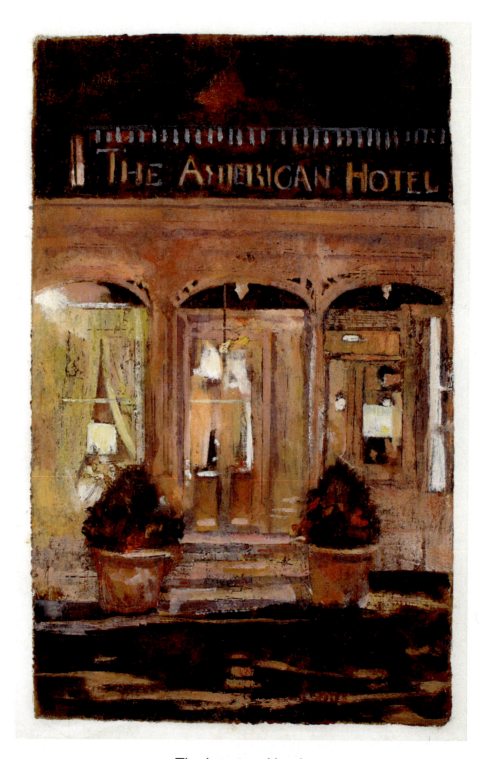

The American Hotel

The hotel remained in their family for almost a hundred years. When Jack's grandfather Will died in 1970 at 94, the family put the hotel up for sale. Two years later on a very cold day, Jack and his brother-in-law met a potential buyer standing at the front door, a very young looking twenty-four year old—Ted Conklin.

Jack Youngs remembered that day:

> We walked through the hotel, got into the lobby, and Ted's eyes are looking and his mind is going off… and we walked into the back room which is now the beautiful bar room with the fireplace… the tin ceiling is kind of falling down. Ted says, "We can do this, we can do that, we can move this over there." My brother-in-law and I are looking at each other, saying this guy is crazy, Man. It's 1972, it's a blue-collar town, there's no one around except the workers at the watchcase factory. Who is going to come to this place?

Ted rolled up his sleeves and fixed up the entire hotel. Period wallpapers, antique furniture, an award-winning wine cellar and the hotel quickly became the place to go for drinks and dinner. The hotel continues to be a destination at the center of Sag Harbor's Main Street and is still owned by the original Ted Conklin.

Doris Gronlund is part of a group that she first referred to as "little old ladies." She quickly corrected that and said, "The ladies who lunch," who go to the hotel once a month. "One of them said it was too expensive, and I said 'Who are you saving the money for?'"

To the left of the front porch of the hotel is a little shop that has housed many different businesses. For many years it was Carruther's Florist. Doris said, "That was something; what an experience to go in and buy flowers. You always got fresh flowers from Ency Beyer and her mother, Mrs. Carruthers."

Oh, That's Another Story

American Hotel parlor

6

Gas Stations

In the 1930s, Jim McMahon, had a moving business in the barn next door to the building which a short time later became Harbor Heights gas station. On the eve of World War II, Jim realized that it would help the moving business to have a steady supply of gasoline and bought the gas station. Jack Van Kovics, Jim's grandson, related this tale, "Part of the start of the trucking business had to do with prohibition, especially from the east end of Long Island to Manhattan." Laughing, he continues, "It's only a story. There is no criminal record, no way to prove this really happened!" In 1954, Jack's father, Van van Kovics, figured the demand for coal wasn't going to last and they ought to buy a fuel oil truck, a big investment. To afford it, teenage Jack, his mother and two friends ran Paul Scheerer's ice cream store, the Cream Queen, on Montauk Highway all summer. "You can make a lot of money [selling ice cream] if you don't mind working twelve hours a day, seven days a week," said Jack. They made enough to buy the truck.

According to Jack, there once were seven garages in Sag Harbor at the same time. If you counted the gas pumps in front of grocery stores and the bicycle shop there could have been even more. Harbor

Oh, That's Another Story

Heights in the 1970s still had its Pegasus sign, the mythical red horse with wings, on the wall, and charge accounts. Filling up meant a chance to chat with Pam Kern, fabled blond lady of the pumps, affectionately known as "the Queen of 114," who knows everyone and everything happening in Sag Harbor. In winter you could wait for your car to be serviced relaxing in an old arm chair in front of the coal stove with the newspaper and be treated to the latest Sag Harbor tales.

For years there was an old swallowtailed dray parked at Harbor Heights. It was a two-wheeled horse-drawn cart originally used to deliver goods in barrels shipped into Long Wharf. When horses were still seen on local streets the dray was also used to pick up the dead ones. They were hauled out of the village and dumped in the woods south of the village. Mary Lee North Egusquiza said she spent lots of time exploring when she was a kid. "We would come across the old wooden wheels with the spokes, and old cow bones and stuff. There were old carts … and big bones."

In the early part of the twentieth century as more automobiles were produced filling stations popped up all over the village with many downtown on Main Street. John Ward told us, "Just about half the stores had gas pumps out front: one at Joe Parker's at Hampton and Jermain, one outside Youngs's Bicycle shop on Main, and there was a garage near the Corner Bar that had a pump out front." Robert Browngardt recalled, "You could drive your car straight in."

On Main Street's west side there was a Texaco station at the foot of the bridge, replaced in the 1980s by a new retail building, known around town as Fort Apache for its U-shaped fortress aura. The Shell station at Nassau St., owned by Danny McLane Jr. and his brother Bill, was converted to a restaurant, currently known as Muse. At Alippo's, a few doors south, Mrs. Alippo served spaghetti on the left side of the building and her husband pumped Sinclair Dino gasoline from the other side, now a surf shop. Robert Browngardt said, "Mrs. Alippo would spit on her frying pan to make sure it was hot!" This made a huge impression on her customers and the story is still repeated decades later.

Further away from downtown, near Mashashimuet Park, was Johnny Peters's Flying A station, and George Ward's Mobil station. Len Heinrich's earlier Mobil has since become a snack bar, then a bakery and now the Bay Burger. Beyond that was Ken Fleishman's Sunoco, now the Fireplace Store.

Today only three garages remain, all on the outskirts of the village and as of this writing only two pump gas.

Gas Stations

Harbor Heights

7

Bars and Restaurants

There were plenty of luncheonettes and lunch counters in Sag Harbor while the factories were going strong. Ted Proferes's Paradise Restaurant had a long counter with stools on the left and booths running the length of the store on the right. It was the place that stayed open until 10 pm so moviegoers could get a bite before heading home. In the 1990s it evolved from sodas and burgers to a dinner menu but still served comfort food. Their meatloaf and mashed potatoes were classic.

On red checked table cloths, Il Capuccino serves up Italian-American fare such as delicious mussels and rolls dripping in garlic, oil, and parsley. Guaranteeing a robust meal seven days a week and all through the winter, Il Cap is still packed with locals, a warm refuge on a cold snowy night.

In the 1950s Il Cap was called Anthony's and a plate of spaghetti was $3.00. Overhead baskets of red faux geraniums dripped with hanging ivy. Anthony was short of help one night, so he asked one of the younger regulars, Rocco Liccardi, to wait tables. "I said, Anthony, I can't do this, I'm too tall…too awkward." It was pouring rain and Anthony put down layers of newspaper to soak up the puddles. "A man by himself walks in, wearing a yellow slicker. 'Where do I sit?' Take the bloom with the view, I said. He

Oh, That's Another Story

Il Capuccino Ristorante

sat by the window. He laughed because every time I came to his table my hair got stuck in the geranium vines and he helped me get untangled. And the squishing of the newspapers was terrible. Now, this is the catch. As he was leaving I apologized to him and said 'What was that you were writing?' He said my name is Craig Claiborne. He gave Anthony three stars in the New York Times. You could not park in Sag Harbor from that time until Anthony closed." Today, Il Capuccino in the same red building, has expanded into two little buildings next door, including the Art Stall seen on page 110 restored with its original quirky facade by current owner Jack Tagliasacchi.

Rumor has it that Sag Harbor once had twenty-seven bars. The count today maxes out at sixteen, still a good number for such a small town. In the whaling days, rum was the drink of choice. In fact, indentured sailors were paid in rum. The Black Buoy, founded by Rose and Jim Black, was legendary in the 1960s and several generations of restaurants have since filled its space. Remembering the Black Buoy, the late Russ Eberhardt said, "Sonia was the bar maid who was a total surprise to any outsider. She did the *New York Times* crossword puzzle every day while she was working the bar and serving drinks. She had a vocabulary that was unbelievable and, at the same time, she could turn around and undress you very nicely—verbally."

Fred Abelman recalled, "Sonia kept that diary of stuff and she had a lot of Black Buoy memorabilia." To confirm the Black Buoy's status as infamous, we heard the tale of two guys who decided to add a Sag Harbor twist to the art of streaking. Calling it "snailing," they disrobed and sauntered slowly about the bar—some say on the bar—and maybe even raced across the street to the American Hotel where they would have been met with Ted Conklin's strict dress code. Cappy Amundsen, renowned marine artist, was a regular at the pool table in the back room of the Black Buoy.

Sal and Joe's was another popular spot. Gabe Schiavoni told us, "It was just a bar where my uncle was a bookie. We called him Uncle Buck, Buckshot. His name was Guido. He never worked." Shown a photo of him we see a handsome man of evident charm.

Oh, That's Another Story

The Corner Bar

An ad in the *Sag Harbor Express* in 2013 celebrating their thirty-fifth anniversary, said it all:

The Corner Bar, Sag Harbor: Still Pre-Existing and Non-Conforming.

These terms, usually used to describe historic buildings and their special status in the zoning code, suit the owners and patrons of The Corner Bar. Known as McLane's in the post-prohibition 1930s, the Corner overlooks the harbor and is a mainstay of the village. John Ward told us, "For my father, before he got sick, I used to go down to McLane's for a bucket of beer for 15 cents. They didn't have bottled beer or nothing in them days. You had to go someplace where they had it on draft. The bucket had a little lid on it. I didn't know what was in it! McLane owned that bar. The building was two stories and was ten feet out further in the street. When they built the new bridge the street was widened and they had to cut the building back, left the top off, and built the new bar. I used to go down there, had a hamburger, soda, cup of tea or something for about a quarter, and you couldn't eat half of it. That's the way things used to be."

Bars and Restaurants

Murf's Backstreet Tavern

The late Tom Murphy opened Murf's in 1976 and ran the old fashioned pub for thirty-one years. Locals and anyone who wanted to relax or have a rowdy time were welcome. The building is a classic Sag Harbor half-house, a type built from the 1790s into the next century, found throughout the village. With a door and two windows on the front facade, these houses were framed by carpenters who would be familiar with shipbuilding techniques of the time. The interior walls have been removed, exposing the early wood posts and beams, and the original fireplace is still there. Here, on the backside of Main Street, is a rare survivor of Sag Harbor's many downtown fires. Murf's remains a rustic and friendly setting for a beer, game of darts, or the devilishly difficult pirates' ring toss, perhaps a local invention.

Oh, That's Another Story

Classics

8

Cinema and Theater

The Art Deco sign in glowing neon on the Sag Harbor Cinema reads simply: Sag Harbor. It has been a beacon on Main Street since 1936 and has become the famous subject of many artists and photographers. The drama to save it was equal to the film dramas shown within. In the early 2000s after the letters S, A, and G had burnt out, and the metal brackets were lacy with corrosion, the sign was taken down in pieces. Destined for the dump, it was to be replaced by a plastic sign that was similar but definitely not the original. The morning the workers arrived and started dismantling the first few letters, an energetic filmmaker emerged from her yoga class across the street, saw what was happening and got on her cell phone. In no time, the community rallied and saved all the pieces. Over the next few months enough money was raised to ensure the cinema owner could provide a replica of the old sign with the same iconic brilliance of the original. Today, the cinema with its new sign has been listed as a registered historic landmark in the local zoning code.

In the 1940s and '50s children flocked to the movies without their parents. "I was there as a little girl. Twenty-five cents! And I vaguely remember Mrs. Eldredge who had played the piano for silent film,"

Oh, That's Another Story

Sag Harbor Cinema

recalled Ann Yardley Hansen. Dorothy Zaykowski remembered, "Mrs. Eldredge, I think she played in the Presbyterian Church, too. But Howard, her husband… she used to push him downstreet in a wicker wheelchair and I think that wheelchair is still in the church's collection." Diane Schiavoni added to the story: when passing by the house, "I used to see her playing the piano in the nude! Her boobs were hanging down. Oh, she played piano beautifully!" And about the wheelchair, "He would get in it and she would push it. When they got to a curb he would get out and she would push the chair back on the sidewalk and she would get in it. They would switch!"

For the bicentennial celebration, Joe Markowski asked Mrs. Eldredge to play the piano for the silent movie, *Down to the Sea in Ships*. "She had never seen the movie and did a fantastic job!" added Joe. The Eldredges continued to go to the movies long after the talkies had eliminated her job as the accompanist. She and Howard sat in the front row where they provided a running commentary out loud to the merriment of the rest of audience. During the film Mrs. Eldredge would say, "Howard, can I have a peanut?" Rocco Liccardi related. "It was more fun to listen to the Eldredges than watch the movie."

Mrs. Eldredge is one of several odd inspirations for this book. She and Howard were the prior owners of Whitney and Peter Hansen's house on Rogers Street. Howard tuned and repaired pianos and the basement was full of piano parts when the Hansens bought it. Down the street another building was called the Piano House where he sold pianos. Howard Eldredge had a horse, a prized trotter, that he kept in a little barn that is now Whitney's studio. John Ward told us, "In the winter when the weather was really cold, Howie would bring the horse inside the house to keep him warm."

There have been movie theaters in Sag Harbor since 1908 when the Montauk Motion Picture Theatre opened on Washington Street across from the watchcase factory. Later incarnations were the Elite and Glynn's Sag Harbor Theatre which introduced the first talking/sound pictures in 1930. This building was torn down and replaced in 1936 and the Sag Harbor Theatre reopened, replete with art deco details and crystal chandeliers. Now known as the Sag Harbor Cinema, its interior still has that slightly musty antique aroma accompanied by an occasional clank from the radiators. Candy and popcorn are sold in the lobby but the films today are often foreign or independent, along with the cream of Hollywood.

Mrs. Eldredge's Wheelchair

When Nada Barry, long the owner of the Wharf Shop, related her experience at the movies. She remembered, "When I was a teenager, seventeen or eighteen, going in there and being shunted to the side because I was a child and all the children had to sit on one side of that movie house. You didn't just sit elsewhere, so they could chaperone you. Having grown up in London and New York, I was shocked! The first time I dated a local person and was on Main Street the next day … the barber was sitting outside and he said, 'How was your evening with so-and-so?' Holy Smoke, what a shock—living in a small town!" Nada also recalled going to the movies in East Hampton. She attended a dance camp run by Anita Zahn, a pupil of Isadora Duncan, in a big house on Lily Pond Lane. "There was one black student

Oh, That's Another Story

Bay Street Theatre

and when Miss Zahn wanted to take us all to the movies in East Hampton she had to call up to see if she would be allowed to bring a black child with the others. This was in the 1940s!"

In the late 1980s three friends met for lunch on Sag Harbor's Main Street and, looking across at the old Grumman factory, they decided to start a theatre. The late Sybil Christopher, Emma Walton, and her husband Steve Hamilton had deep connections in the theatre world. Emma had known Sybil since childhood. Emma's father, Tony Walton, is a set designer and her mother, Julie Andrews, was playing opposite Richard Burton in the musical *Camelot* on Broadway not long before Emma was born. Sybil Christopher was married to Richard Burton at the time and had had an earlier career as an actress. She later opened a famous discotheque called Arthur in New York City. She may have been aware that day at lunch that there had been a short-lived disco in the empty factory space.

For its premier play in 1992 The Bay Street Theatre presented *Men's Lives*, written by local playwright Joe Pintauro based on the book by Peter Matthiessen of the same title. Matthiessen had been a resident of nearby Sagaponack for many years and his nonfiction work is based on the commercial fishermen of this area. The enduring conflict between the men, the environment, and government regulations is told as personal stories, some in their own Bonac accents inherited from generations of English forebears.

The theatre has become a cultural center for the village, presenting plays, films, live music, a comedy club, and providing summer internships and theater camp for children.

9

Social Clubs, Civic Organizations, Fire Department

The Sag Harbor Golf Club was long famous for its oiled sand greens and laid-back club-house bar. Acquired in 1989 by New York State, the greens are grass but the management is still run by local residents and the ambience remains relaxed. The Club was founded by a group of Sag Harbor residents on the old LaGuire dairy farm in the early 1900s in the area now known as Barcelona Point. The early members pooled their money to buy the land and each member took on the care of one green. Not long afterward the club disbanded. In 1929 a group of Sag Harbor men learned that the property was once again for sale and resuscitated the golf club. The four-hundred-acre property was purchased in November of that year and renovation of the abandoned course began the following February. Once the snow had melted the members burned the overgrown fairways and built the first green from clay mixed with sand. The contract to remove trees, construct the new nine-hole course, and improve the road went to James McMahon Jr. By now this is a name familiar to the reader—a man who never overlooked an opportunity.

Oh, That's Another Story

Sag Harbor Golf Club

There have been two small clubhouses at the top of the hill. One that burned in the early 1930s was replaced in 1933 by the existing club house. For many years the clay-and-sand greens were still treated with oil and rolled to keep them smooth. In the 1980s a group of Sag Harbor residents, among them the noted Nancy Boyd Willey and Carol Williams, were concerned with the preservation of the remaining three-hundred-forty-one acres, hoping to save it from development. "Save Barcelona" bumper stickers graced the backs of pickup trucks and workers' vans, prompting out-of-towners to wonder what was happening in Spain. By 1989 the group succeeded and Barcelona Point was taken over by New York State. Today the Sag Harbor State Golf Course continues to be operated by the Sag Harbor Golf Club for the public with traditionally inexpensive memberships and very low fees to anyone who wants to play. It remains an informal spot for a card game and a beer even on rainy days.

A moving postscript to the golf club story is the renaming of the state's land as the Linda Gronlund Memorial Nature Preserve at Barcelona Neck, in memory of Doris Gronlund's daughter who died in the crash of Flight 93 in Pennsylvania on September 11, 2001. Doris came to Sag Harbor fifty years ago when her husband was an executive with Sag Harbor Industries. Their families were Norwegian from

Sag Harbor Yacht Club

Bay Ridge in Brooklyn. Doris always worked, starting as a wholesale buyer in New York City, dealing in toys, clothing, and fabrics. "Then I went to International Milling Co. at 11 Broadway. I became assistant to the executive v. p. and learned how to buy wheat. My mom said when you talk to a man you have to give him your idea so he thinks he thought it up." She added, "My mother taught me how to stretch a dollar until it squeaked. I made so much money in the fifties. Betty Friedan said I should have been in her book." For years Doris was the proprietor of a large local clothing store that she purchased from Russell Basile in 1972. She called it Sagalund and carried a varied inventory, work pants, and shirts in green, gray, and tan, J. M. Herman workboots, as well as white dress shirts and ties. "I always listened to my customers, never any merchandise too loud."

The Sag Harbor Yacht Club, founded 1899, is the combination of two earlier clubs. The Volunteer Boat Club was for smaller boats that could fit through the drawbridge to reach the shallower waters of the cove. The Harbor Yacht Club was for larger boats east of the bridge in the open harbor. The new Sag Harbor Yacht Club spent a few years west of Long Wharf and, in 1913, moved to its current location on Bay Street. Today's clubhouse was originally built on Shelter Island by the New York Yacht Club and floated from the island to the harbor in 1914 and was installed on the club's new dock.

Oh, That's Another Story

Sailors compete for the Maycroft Cup, Havens Cup, and Ron Lowe Cup Regattas each season and impressive powerboats crowd the docks. The Sag Harbor Yacht Club's membership is limited by the number of slips and they are rarely relinquished, with a long waiting list. Numerous marinas have dock space, two east of Long Wharf on either side of the yacht club and several under the bridge in Sag Harbor Cove. A public launching ramp is on Bay Street; bait, fishing gear, and boat services are available nearby at the Sag Harbor Yacht Yard.

A relatively new club is the not-for-profit Breakwater Yacht Club on Bay Street, established to provide sailing lessons for young people and adults. It also sponsors sailing races, and encourages and prepares the Sag Harbor community to partake of and enjoy the waters of Sag Harbor. Their Wednesday night and Sunday races are highly competitive. After the races, salty captains and crews go to various waterfront establishments to drink to the winners and celebrate. The new clubhouse looks out on the harbor and is a fine venue for community meetings and private events.

Private or exclusive clubs have played a minor yet supporting role in the social life of Sag Harbor. The "country clubs" of this area are at some distance, in the resorts of East Hampton and Southampton. Founded before the turn of the twentieth century these clubs are large and maintain golf, tennis, sailing, and beach facilities restricted to members and their guests. Jack van Kovics recalled a family story concerning the Maidstone Club in East Hampton, "My grandmother was French. She came over here from France as a lady's helper, decided she didn't like it, came out here with a friend to work at the Maidstone Club. Historically, the Maidstone Club employees have these parties after service is over, beach parties. My grandfather, Jim McMahon, met my grandmother at one of those parties on the beach."

In his childhood recollections published in 1987 Robley Logan describes attending a boy scout camp near Montauk Manor. "The latter facility provided us as caddies for the local Montauk Downs Golf Course, each of us pocketing our own round earnings, and paying thirty dollars a month for room and board, a profitable venture for us as well as a valuable experience." He further explains that later, with the Depression, those jobs went to married men.

The only local club that might have been considered "elitist" was the Sag Harbor Lawn and Tennis Club on Redwood, then called Brush Neck, the estate of a Dr. Morton. In the 1890s the good doctor dedicated some of his property for grass tennis courts. Though most of the tennis players were the children of the wealthier Sag Harbor families—the Aldriches, Fahyses, Cooks, Mortons, Napiers, Sleights, and Sterlings—the rest of the area was used as a park by the Sag Harbor community.

The American Legion is located directly across from the two yacht clubs on Bay Street. Legion meetings are held in the left side of this building and, in summer, the Sag Harbor Community Band sets up on the terrace every Tuesday night for free concerts of old-fashioned music. Families bring their own chairs, picnic suppers, drink coolers and take over the street. The right side and a portion of the rear of

Social Clubs, Civic Organizations, Fire Department

The American Legion Chelberg and Battle Post 388

the building is rented to the Dockside Bar and Grill, a popular restaurant and bar and casual hang out for year-rounders and summer folk with a great view of the boats in the harbor.

Once upon a time, a little engine house sat on the bank of Otter Pond, facing Main Street. The Otter Hose Company was one of five fire companies located throughout the village, all part of the Sag Harbor Fire Department. After Mrs. Russell Sage created Mashashimuet Park in 1909, she added the land around Otter Pond to the park and demolished or gave away the buildings on the pond shore. She suggested that the engine house be moved across Main Street onto the only open space available, a little road called Willow Street which the Village trustees had just decommissioned. Ironically, a raging fire consumed the engine house in 1912 and it was immediately replaced by the firehouse that is there today.

The new home for the Otter Hose Company once had a huge bar upstairs and space for one fire truck at ground level. Wet canvas hoses were hung to dry in a tall tower at the back of the building. In 1974 it was sold to Dick and Tucker Burns Roth who turned it into a private residence. The big wooden bar was

Oh, That's Another Story

Otter Hose Company

removed at the time of the sale but its fame lives on. "We had a lot of good times in that firehouse. There was a painting over the bar. It was taken out by the boys," said John Ward.

Chartered in 1803, the Sag Harbor Fire Department is one of the oldest in New York State. With Sag Harbor's warehouses containing grain, whale oil, and other combustibles on the wharf, the village had the added disadvantage of steady north winds off the water that would sweep a small fire right up Main Street into a giant conflagration. Many raging fires changed the face of downtown over the course of the nineteenth century. To assure that all neighborhoods had fire-fighting equipment nearby the Fire Department distributed the small fire companies throughout the village. Today, two companies still operate on sites distant from the new central firehouse on Columbia Street. The 1899 Murray Hill Hose Company on Henry Street has remained, due to its proximity to the public elementary and high schools. The Phoenix and Gazelle Companies moved in 1916, to share a new building at the center of Main Street between the Municipal Building and the American Hotel. The fire department still throws great parties for its volunteers, steak dinners, all you can eat. They march in parades, compete in tournaments, and maintain a collection of antique trucks and equipment.

The Firemen's Museum, founded in 1978, is housed in a building dating to 1833 on Church and Sage Streets. Originally the Sessions House for the early Presbyterian Church, the building sat directly across the street from the current location. Sold when the Old Whalers' Church was built in 1844, it became the Village Hall, complete with a jail in its stone cellar. "At one time the temperance ladies met there, [protesting] against bootlegging, and the fire department kept a truck there," according to John Ward. Not long ago a woman visiting the museum asked John about the early firecarts that were pulled by men who ran all the way to the fire, "'Where were the horses?' she asked. I said, 'Home with the wives.'"

Set at the southern edge of Sag Harbor, Mashashimuet Park was given its Algonquin name by local historian William Wallace Tooker. It means "at the great spring," for the fresh-water springs just east of the park that feed Otter Pond. In the nineteenth century a fairgrounds existed where the park now stands, with a half-mile track for trotting races and an exhibition building for agricultural competitions for the best vegetables, farm animals, flower arranging, and especially pie. A last burst of enthusiasm for cycling brought over a thousand people to the track for a race in the gay 1890s. By the turn of the twentieth century more local people were involved in factory work than farming, horses were replaced by cars, and the fairgrounds were neglected.

Mrs. Russell Sage began her extraordinary philanthropy in Sag Harbor in 1908 when she donated the new Pierson School and the John Jermain Memorial Library to the community. At a picnic that same year she became concerned by the sad state of the local fairgrounds and purchased the property to build a park. Within the next two years the land was transformed under her supervision. Truckloads of topsoil were brought from a farm in nearby Bridgehampton, a ball field was created inside the old race track oval, and a grandstand was built for spectators. The park manager's house and a house for rainy-day activities for children were built and four tennis courts installed. The next year Mrs. Sage extended the park to the north, purchasing all the lots around Otter Pond, moving several houses, donating some

Oh, That's Another Story

Mashashimuet Park Gate

to the needy and tearing down others. Her vision and the mission statement for the park was "exclusively charitable, benevolent, and patriotic, being the mental and physical development and improvement of children and young people." At this time the fate of child workers in a factory town would be on Mrs. Sage's mind. Ten years later, not long after her death, the United States Congress passed a child labor law but it was declared unconstitutional. The Fair Labor Standards Act which set the minimum age for children working during the school day at sixteen years old, after school jobs at fourteen, and dangerous work at age eighteen, wasn't enacted until 1938.

The park provides ball fields for the local schools and local athletic organizations, a playground, and a public tennis program on ten tennis courts. The southern end of the Park abuts the Long Pond Greenbelt, an enormous tract of land full of kettlehole ponds and nature trails stretching from Sag Harbor to Bridgehampton. Most of this land has been acquired and protected for public use. Mrs. Sage set up the park as a not-for-profit corporation. As such, Mashashimuet Park supports itself with the proceeds of the tennis program, contracting the use of playing fields by the school district, and through charitable donations.

Social Clubs, Civic Organizations, Fire Department

Mashashimuet Park Playground

Everyone we interviewed had fond memories of the park from the time they spent in the playground to participating in school sports, to the Sag Harbor Athletic League softball games between competing local businesses. William Pickens, III, a summer resident of Eastville, recalled playing stickball with a "Spaldeen," that pink rubber ball made by Spaulding, against the wall of the grandstand. "We'd take our bikes and come down the dirt road to the park. We played ball there a lot." Fred Abelman remembered it, too, "A tree out there was a triple, it was a double if you got somewhere else. The grandstand is a special place." The strike zone painted white on the brick wall in the 1940s is still there. The grandstand itself offers a view of the baseball field and shelter from the elements. The UPS men have gathered and eaten their lunch there on rainy days for years.

Patricia Archibald's grandparents owned a large tract of land next to the park. Her father divided it into housing lots and put in the street called Archibald's Way in the early 1990s. Patti said, "That's my park! When we were kids we thought we owned it. My grandmother actually told us we did," and they believed her.

Oh, That's Another Story

The Grandstand Strike Zone

The park manager's house, built on a hill in the simple shingle style a hundred years ago, has an ample porch with a view of Otter Pond. From the Depression and through the 1960s the park house was rented to local families whose kids relished their huge "backyard." Judy McGowin Lattanzio's mother Earle and her aunt Elizabeth grew up in the park house in the 1930s. "My grandparents, Redfield and Earle Wright, lived there, and my grandfather was on the park board for years." Judy continues the family's connection to the park by serving on their board of directors today.

Larry and Ida Abelman, already mentioned in the story of the Bottle House, lived in the park house from 1952 to 1970. Margaret Abelman Bromberg and her brother Fred related the story of their parents' arrival in Sag Harbor in 1945. "My father worked in the Brooklyn Navy yard and with the war winding down he decided to take a summer vacation in Sag Harbor which was a village," said Margaret. A small scale, closely knit neighborhood was important as they were "city people," didn't have a car, and wanted to be able to walk everywhere. Fred added, "After a few days Dad called his boss, 'This is a great place. Can we take a couple more weeks?' 'Yeah,' says the boss, 'take two weeks.'" Those weeks stretched into the fall. Larry Abelman got ready to go back to work. When he finally reached his boss again, the answer was, "There is no job." Larry then went to work for his Sag Harbor landlord, Charles Malles, and became a wholesaler of vegetables, making deliveries throughout the area.

Larry's wife Ida was an accomplished artist. Many of her artist friends moved in the 1940s to Springs, a rural area further east on the island. For her, Sag Harbor's urban setting would be better for raising her children. The kids quickly got to know the village. "Every neighborhood had a market, related to our father's business," said Margaret. "We went to Diste's (then Distefano's, now the Cove Deli) on Main

Mashashimuet in Winter

Street. It was the closest when we lived in the park house. We stopped for candy at Johnny and Eddie's on our way to school and there was a disastrous fire that burned the top off their building when we were kids." Ida Abelman kept up with her artist friends and her daughter Margaret's husband, Michael Bromberg, related this story: "They had a party at the park house. Jackson Pollock got very drunk and drove out the driveway into Otter Pond. And, Ida, who wouldn't even hang her laundry where a neighbor could see it, was so offended that she banned him from any further parties. Ida, being the wit she was, later said she thought that 'Pollock were found in deeper waters.'"

Mashashimuet Park is an old-fashioned place. The playground is a casual mix of swings, seesaws, and handmade rocking boats. More modern structures have arrived with fanfare and, after years of use, disappeared. A large climbing rock, brand new and totally artificial, looks like the real thing under the oak trees. The rocking animals have to be repaired from time to time, but have been here since the 1960s and are still revered.

Joe Burns, former park manager, recalls an incident he calls Chicken-Gate. In an email he had this to say: "I thought someone had taken our bouncing chicken from the park and dumped him at either

Oh, That's Another Story

Otter Pond at Christmas

Long Wharf or behind Murf's Tavern. I do know the police came to the park's shop, opened their trunk, and showed me a very contrite and exhausted springy capon. I told the officer that he was indeed our wayward fowl and swore that he would never roam again." Joe spent twenty-two years as the benevolent overseer of the park and the people who enjoy it, their praise following in his quiet wake. Incidentally, our contemporary Joe Burns is a direct descendant of the Joseph Burns who came to work at the watch-case factory in the 1880s.

10

Schools

Public education for the first half of the nineteenth century in Sag Harbor took place in several school houses like this one on Division near Henry Street. It was the third school house to be built and after a short time the structure was moved up the street to this location and later converted to a residence. In prosperous whaling times there were also private schools and classes taught in private homes.

In 1862 Sag Harbor's three public school districts were combined into one, the Union School District. The Mansion House, a hotel on Main Street, was purchased in 1871 for use as the Union School. By the turn of the twentieth century, New York State threatened to condemn the old Union School and the village was desperate for a new school house. Mrs. Russell Sage came to the rescue in 1907, providing funds for a new building on Division Street to be named after her mother's ancestors, the Piersons. The Union School was then acquired by the village for use as the Municipal Building.

When the cornerstone for the new Pierson school was laid, two hundred students marched from the old school in a long line to the new site. Close to two thousand people gathered for the dedication

Oh, That's Another Story

Old School House

ceremonies. A collection of photographs, coins, and lists of all involved with the school at the time were installed in the cornerstone. The Elementary school and Pierson High School have held the community together. Since World War II the divisions between nationalities and religions relaxed as kids had classes together, grew up, and fell in love. Michael Bromberg remarked that his wife Margaret, "went all through school with the same twenty-seven kids and most of them are still here."

Miles Anderson reported to us that during the Depression once a female teacher married she had to give up her job so an unemployed man with a family to support would have work. This lasted until World War II when women took men's places, not just as teachers but in local factories as well.

When Victoria Schiavoni came from Brooklyn in the 1950s to teach at the Pierson High School she needed a place to stay. Mr. Crozier, the principal, asked Angelo Schiavoni (president of the school board) and his wife if Vicki could stay at their house until she found a place of her own. "He called my future mother-in-law. 'I have this young woman coming and she needs a place to stay. Can she stay at your

School House Cupola

house?' 'No, she cannot stay at my house because I'm re-doing my kitchen, my refrigerator is in the back parlor and we are washing dishes in the bathroom sink!'" But he prevailed on her. The Schiavoni's daughter was away, teaching in Center Moriches during the week, and Vicki slept in her room. "In a few days their son Joe was kind enough to drive me around town and find me a little apartment… in a house just down the street… Then he finally got around to asking me out and that was the beginning of it." She found out ten years later that Mr. Crozier had had something more in mind. "He said, 'You know, I played cupid for you.' That's why he insisted that I stay at the home of Mr. and Mrs. Schiavoni. They had two eligible young men and certainly one of them would be interested in me so that I would stay in Sag Harbor and he wouldn't have to look for another teacher the next year."

St. Andrew Roman Catholic Church founded its parochial school in the 1860s in an old building already used by the Episcopalians and Methodists since 1811. It served the children until 1872 when it was cut in two and reassembled on Glover Street as a tenement. A new building took its place and is best remembered by students for its view of the Presbyterian Church during the hurricane of 1938.

Oh, That's Another Story

Municipal Building, formerly the Union School

Schools

The Academy of the Sacred Heart of Mary

Many of the children were still in school the afternoon of the storm. Before the days of radar, satellites, and on-the-minute weather forecasts, this raging storm arrived without warning. Some children ran home alone through the ferocious winds while parents tried to reach them at school. John Cilli, the youngest of seven children, was at Pierson High School that day with his sister Ange. "We were ready to stay at school but my older sister Rose, working at the factory, walked to school to get us," recalled John. "We walked home, climbing over trees…and everything, and then in the water because the street [Glover Street] was under water…. Since there was no electricity, no one had running water. It was such a mess, all at once! The old fire truck, the Maxi, was hooked up to a well in the middle of Main Street. For eight days, they pumped water from that well into the water system and the hydrants."

The first American foundation of the Religious of the Sacred Heart of Mary came to Sag Harbor in 1877. Their academy, a girls' high school for local and boarding students, was housed in a large mansion on Hampton Street. A beautiful chapel was built next door in 1888. Larry Burns said, "The New York City girls were wild and the girls from South America were rich! We boys would climb up in the trees outside and the girls would be upstairs in the convent. We'd be peeking in. I had a friend, Joe. He fell out of a tree and the cop was standing right at the bottom. 'OK, Einstein, I got you right where I want

Oh, That's Another Story

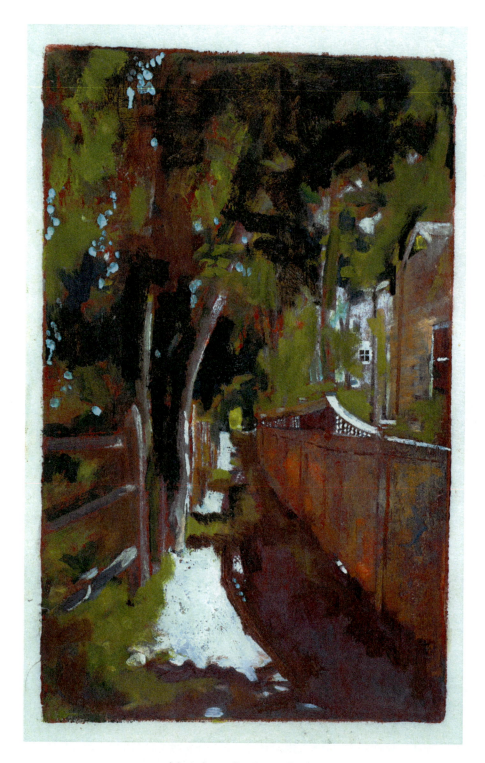

Nuns' or Convent Path

you.' The girls were just as bad as the boys. They were crazy! Wild things went on up there." When the Academy expanded, the mansion and chapel were torn down to make way for the large brick building which now serves as the public elementary school. "It broke my heart," said Larry.

In the 1943, the Religious of the Sacred Heart of Mary purchased the Frank C. Havens house near Havens Beach on the bay, not far from the village. The teaching nuns started a finishing school, a junior college called the Cormaria Institute of Arts and Science in the shingled mansion overlooking the harbor.

The Nuns' or Convent Path was a shortcut for the teachers from the Academy to the swimming beach and Cormaria Institute. In 1946 the nuns' order closed the Institute and used the Havens home as the Cormaria Retreat House. In the twenty-first century the Sisters still run programs in this peaceful and beautiful setting. Joe Markowski remembers a kind of enclosed merry-go-round shower with changing rooms in the basement of that house, probably a holdover from Havens's ownership. The dirt path remains a good shortcut to Havens Beach for the fourth of July fireworks over the harbor.

Patricia Archibald attended all the schools in Sag Harbor in the 1950s. She and her sister went to the Academy of the Sacred Heart of Mary from kindergarten through grade six, then to St. Andrew school for seventh and eighth, and then back to the Academy. "Then I went to Pierson High School so I would be eligible for BOCES Hair Dressing School." (BOCES is the Board of Cooperative Educational Services provided to local school districts, sharing and reducing costs.) Patti continues, "The other day, my sister and I were laughing, how fancy the schools are today. When we went to St. Andrew's in the old wooden building we didn't have a telephone in the school. The teacher asked me to go over to Korsak's Madison Market and ask Mrs. Korsak if we could borrow the phone to call the lady that played the organ so we could practice for Easter. Can you imagine if there was an emergency? Or, I would go across to the church to ask Father Ennis if I could use that phone and he would grumble. He had very bad asthma. He'd get up on the altar and I think the incense would throw him for a loop. He'd choke and choke and get redder and redder. When I asked him if I could use the phone he'd say 'What does that woman want now?'"

11

Library, Book Stores, and Newspapers

The John Jermain Memorial Library (JJML) was another gift of the benevolent Mrs. Russell Sage to the village of Sag Harbor. Completed in 1910 it is named for her grandfather Major John Jermain and was designed in the grand Classical Revival style. To celebrate the 2007 publication of the book, *Voices of Sag Harbor, a Village Remembered*, a great many contributors gathered in the rotunda of the Library under its stained-glass skylight. I remember clearly when Liz Bowser, tall, stately, with soft measured movements, stood to speak. She recalled the rainy days in the 1920s, at age six or seven, when she donned her galoshes and umbrella and walked from Eastville to the library for an afternoon of reading. "It was wonderful to sit in this room, near the window, and hear the rain on the roof."

Dorothy Sherry moved to the village in the early 1960s when Russella Hazard was the librarian at the JJML. "When Linda [Dorothy's daughter] had to do a paper for school on Russia, Miss Hazard wouldn't

Oh, That's Another Story

John Jermain Memorial Library

let her borrow any books on Russia because she was against Russia and the Communist party and everything. She was a wonderful women. The library was her domain and she ruled it with an iron hand."

In 2010, the library celebrated its one-hundredth birthday with a commitment to the restoration of the old building and the addition of a contemporary wing to accommodate expanding library services. The great neoclassical columns still framed the heavy wood entrance doors. Once inside, the walls lined with tall oak bookcases, the matching oak furniture, and the books themselves contributed to the sense of timelessness, solidity, and quiet. In the top floor rotunda the portrait of Major John Jermain remained over the marble fireplace and even the table lamps, photographed at the library's opening, were still in place. Though laced with new bookshelves that projected like tentacles toward the center of the rotunda reading room, the original features of the JJML were unchanged. But it was clear that the JJML needed more space. Every nook and cranny had been stuffed with books, paper work, as well as new media, such as cassettes, videos, and lately CDs and DVDs. The bathrooms were charming with black and white tile floors, but the plumbing was increasingly crotchety. And there were the leaks. The octagonal rotunda was topped by a copper dome with a skylight that filtered daylight through a circle

Canio's Books and Cultural Cafe

of stained glass in the center of the space. It was an astonishingly elegant detail to be found in this factory village, but in time blankets had to be provided to keep the rain off patrons sitting beneath it.

So began the process of committing to change. Meetings, public input, exploring alternatives, and long discussions in many committees resulted finally in community consensus and a plan for the next 100 years. What I can say in one sentence took at least eight years. As of this writing the old building has been painstakingly restored and ground has been broken for a new, modern wing which will wrap around the rear of the building. It is a pleasure to know that the library will continue to change, providing modern services to the village without losing the elegance of a bygone era and the irreplaceable patina that time has bestowed.

Canio Pavone founded his store in 1980 and it has been a lively literary and arts center ever since. The current owners, Maryann Calendrille and Kathryn Szoka, have added Canio's Cultural Cafe, a series of events, writing workshops, and talks. Old books, new books, collectibles, and paperbacks pack the shelves and art exhibitions cover the walls. The audiences for author's readings and art openings squeeze themselves into rows of folding chairs, sit on the floor and stand behind the stacks to listen. At Canio's

Oh, That's Another Story

Books, the art and literary circles of Sag Harbor intersect; in fact, they are seated so close together that it is inevitable that they meet and speak. The building is the epitome of the add-on: a classic Federal house with fan windows is almost completely consumed by the Victorian storefront and a mansard addition with a tower at the back.

The *Sag Harbor Express* newspaper was established in 1859 and later incorporated even earlier papers, the *Sag Harbor News* and the *Corrector*. It has been in print for one-hundred-fifty-plus years and hits the news-stands every Thursday with coverage of local politics, the police blotter, culture and the arts, letters to the editors, editorials, engagements, weddings, and obituaries. Other papers have come and gone, while the *Express* keeps everyone in touch and clarifies the flying rumors that usually precede its weekly publication. Its advertising spreads the word for local businesses and the news is online at www.sagharboronline.com.

Searching for the ambiance of the village, I perused back issues of the *Express* from the 1930s to the '70s on microfiche at the John Jermain Memorial Library. The early front pages are packed with national and international news while local stories show up inside. A column called Village Topics kept track of parties, vacation trips, card games, club meetings, and who was visiting whom. Although Sag Harbor was a true blue-collar factory village, the descriptions of gatherings and entertainments conjure images of women in dresses and high heels comporting themselves with elegance and sophistication. For instance, on January 10, 1930, the paper reported on the Friday Night Bridge Club, consisting of young ladies who were home from various colleges for the holidays. "

> All the students of the N. Y. State Normal Schools and Colleges left Sunday morning January 5th. Miss Margaret Seaton gave a farewell party. Bridge was played followed by dancing and refreshments. Miss Seaton expects to go away and train to be a nurse.

Interspersed among the columns are display ads for local businesses and the classified listings. Scrolling through those old pages is like sauntering down a bygone Main Street. Store after store touts its wares, listing items on sale with prices. And here too, in the depth of the Great Depression, the ads portray a decidedly formal sense of style. "The Kensington Valet Service opposite the American Hotel—Dry Cleaning, Pressing, Tailoring." "Men's Furnishings—George L. McFarland—Suits, Hats, Bostonian Shoes for Men." "Garypie Brothers, Builders of Better Homes." In the classified section under Pianos and Tuning, an ad extols the work of "Stephen Bediance, Expert Restorer and Polisher, Agent for Bosch Radios, Madison Street."

In the 1950s and '60s Sag Harbor suffered the closing of the factories that had supplied equipment for World War II. Instead of a postwar boom, Sag Harbor was slowly losing jobs and searching for new ways to bring back business. Discussions on the running of local government were lengthy and loud but leavened with humor. From the *Sag Harbor Express*, April 16, 1959, near the end of two very long

Library, Book Stores, and Newspapers

Sag Harbor Express

columns relating the heated discussions by the mayor and the village board of trustees as to whom should be on which committee, we have this delightful paragraph from the reporter:

> Lively audience participation in the argument lent color and flavor to the proceedings seldom encountered at Board meetings. Both Mrs. William Lloyd Bassett and Mrs. Douglas Gardner made cogent comments of a political nature which, in the interest of "harmony" had better be skipped. (It's a pity though.)

Mr. Gardner was the editor and publisher of the paper and Mrs. Gardner was Victoria Gardner, his irrepressible wife who succeeded her editor/publisher husband at the paper after his death in January 1960. Mrs. Bassett is JoJo, Josephine O'Halloran Bassett. I remember her as a diminutive and very pretty lady of a certain age who lived with her sister on Madison Street. In the 1940s she and a few others formed the Old Sagg Harbour Committee and worked with Governor Charles Edison of New Jersey to save Sag Harbor's U.S. Custom House, the first in New York State. Another member was Nancy Boyd Willey, conservationist, preservationist, and benefactress. In her will Nancy left her mother's home to the Sag Harbor Historical Society. Since 1988 it has been known as the Annie Cooper Boyd House, a museum and the society's headquarters, named for Nancy's mother. Not afraid to speak up in defense of historic Sag Harbor, Nancy was a thorn in the side of some local politicians. Former mayor John Ward referred to Nancy as the "Weasel" and included Jojo Bassett when he said, "They gave me lots of trouble!" He grinned as he said this.

Miles Anderson, son of another Old Sagg Harbour Committee member, Anita Anderson, had this to say about the ladies, "Do you have tender ears? I have always been terribly amused by the Ladies Village Improvement, and Sag Harbor preservation, and the Old Sagg Harbour Committee. I'm convinced, during the whaling era, Sag Harbor was cat houses and saloons. That was it! Everybody romanticizes that it was all muslins and silk top hats. Hogwash! Probably my great grandfather [Edgar Miles], the doctor here, mostly treated cases of the clap!"

Every week the *Express* compiles a short column called "Yesterday's Express" and reprints the brief notes that appeared in the paper seventy-five, fifty and twenty-five years ago. Even though I may not know the people mentioned, these short tidbits remind me of the tempo and flavor of that Sag Harbor. From the March 10, 1988 issue:

> Many of the yards have daffodils up. Mrs. Joseph Labrozzi's are up about four inches. Little happenings seem so important. Shirley and Win Ruppel's crocuses are up and blooming.

Although there is no byline this sounds like Victoria Gardner who ran the paper until it was purchased by Gardner "Pat" Cowles in 1988. Vickie seemed to fling the paper together with gusto. Big photos spread across the front page were not always perfectly centered or aligned and sometimes a name was spelled one way at the beginning of an article and another toward the end. At the same time, she was always out and about, keeping up with the latest happenings, and her rendering of the news still prompts a smile. She once hired Rocco Liccardi to write a gossip column. "Anything you handed her she would print, including a personal invitation I sent her for a party I was giving!"

12

Antique Shops and Art Galleries

During the 1950s and '60s people from New York City were drawn to Sag Harbor for what it wasn't. It was not high society going to country clubs, nor formal. It was a bit shabby and it definitely was not chic. Artists, writers, and publishers found affordable second homes here. In a village used to the excesses of rowdy whalers and boisterous celebrations by crowds of factory workers, a bunch of city Bohemians fit in easily.

At the time, Sag Harbor's collection of late eighteenth- and nineteenth-century houses was larger than any town in New York State and was largely untouched due to lack of funds. The houses may have needed paint but the original windows, doorways and interior woodwork were usually intact. Their new owners went to work to preserve and restore the old homes and furnish them without spending too much. The local antique shops had the range of prices and the right look—a relaxed formality, yet suited to elegant nineteenth-century proportions and style.

Oh, That's Another Story

Glad Hand Shop Sign

Lovelady Powell, actress, and her partner Peggy White, fashion model, came to Sag Harbor in the 1960s, moving their New York City antique shop to a barn on Church Street. A bit later they purchased The Glad Hand building, a beautiful brick structure, on Madison Street. "A man by the name of Jim Flynn owned it. He was from the city and dealt in maritime artifacts. We talked to Jim and we made a deal, and we got the best end of that deal. He was a very interesting Irishman but he was nuttier than a fruitcake. Jim also owned the most exquisite boat, a 37-foot Hubert Johnson from the Scott Fitzgerald era, all mahogany, just fabulous. He didn't have to but he threw the boat in with the deal."

With the help of close friend and antique dealer Richard Camp, Lovey and Peggy imported antique pine furniture from England and the Netherlands, making the trip to Europe each year to fill a shipping container with old pine breakfronts, welsh cupboards, chests, and tables. "We had a wonderful time in those days."

Across the street from The Glad Hand, New York photographers Otto Fenn and John Krug opened Sag Harbor Antiques. They bought and restored the ancient David Hand house on Church Street behind their Main Street store. Otto and John were early and fervent supporters of historic preservation in Sag Harbor. Otto was on the commission that laid the groundwork for the first Historic District at the time of the 1976 national bicentennial and his photographs were a vital part of the commission's report. The couple were also noted for their cooking and entertaining. A highlight was the spirited eggnog they made for the Ladies Village Improvement Society Christmas House Tour each year. Diane Schiavoni, a long time member of the LVIS, remembers it well: "John would make it in November or October. I know he made it at least a month in advance. He'd stir it once a day. We could only serve it in those tiny paper cups (it was so strong). People came just for that!"

Antique Shops and Art Galleries

Sage Street Antiques

Hal McKusick, a noted 1950s jazz sax player and music teacher, had the Little Barn Antiques shop around the corner on Sage Street. The main house had belonged to actor Hurd Hatfield, who starred in the movie *The Picture of Dorian Gray*. Once a manse for the Presbyterian Church, Hal carefully restored it and filled it with antiques. There were young squirrels living there too, in a crockery pitcher on his fireplace mantel. Hal had found a nest of orphaned babies and brought them inside to raise them. Once when we were using his dining room as a photography location I had a real shock. As I was looking through the camera, a little squirrel ran up my back to my shoulder and then sat there for a moment. On summer days when the windows were open you could hear Hal practicing the sax or giving someone lessons in his front parlor, those mellows notes floating out onto the street.

Just twenty-one years old Rocco Liccardi, opened his first shop, the Black Afghan, on Main Street. (He named the shop for his dog but it elicited lots of questions and comments). An artist, Rocco started out trying to sell just his own paintings. "I painted like crazy. I had so many paintings. In 1961, Mrs. Russuck had a liquor store in Latham House. So many stores were closed, boarded up, and she wanted $75 a month rent. Oh my God, $75. If I could sell just one painting a month I could pay the rent. Well, I never did. Then this Jewish girlfriend, Lucille Saddler, a stained glass artist… she said, 'Rocco, you are

Oh, That's Another Story

The Art Stall

going to starve to death. Tomorrow I am coming with my little boy and lots of tchotchkes.' I thought they were Jewish cookies! Oh boy, this is great. She comes with her old car, opens the trunk and it is full of all this junk: three dishes, a lamp with no shade. I says, 'Do you want me to go to the dump?' She says, 'No, these are the tchotchkes, these are going to pay your rent!' And that's how I began in the antiques business."

Sage Street Antiques opened in this little outbuilding in 1979 while owner Eliza Werner raised her family in the house next door. Later when her kids were grown she moved the shop into the main floor of the house. Equipped with an excellent eye and energy, she spends weekdays searching for furniture, lamps, art, and accessories. For years she has been seen at every yard sale, estate sale, and auction in the area. Open only on Saturdays and Sundays, the shop's line of regular customers can stretch to the street before the door is unlocked. Many bring coffee and chat while they wait.

Artists have come to the East End of Long Island for the light, the big open skies over the vast potato fields and, in time, art galleries followed. In Sag Harbor the first business to hang paintings was the Wharf Shop. When she opened in 1968, Nada Barry stocked high-quality educational children's toys, such as big maple building blocks in their natural finish. Since she knew artists and there weren't any galleries in the village to show their work, she made room for them on the walls of her store.

The Art Stall's odd little building has had a varied past: a laundromat, a piano tuner's shop, a garage, and it might have been a carriage repair shop early on. At the time of this painting in the 1970s, it was occupied by a folk artist, Warren J. McHugh, who carved and painted figures, old salts and sailors, and fish—all things related to the old whaling days and the sea.

In the 1990s when Jack Tagliasacchi planned to expand his Il Capuccino Ristorante next door, he built a connection to this building and carefully restored its fancy facade and big windows. Jack is also an artist and displays his paintings in his restaurant.

One of Sag Harbor's memorable artists, C. Hjalmar Amundsen (1911–2001), aka Cappy, was revered not only for his marine art—exceptional paintings of ships and the sea—but as a colorful local character. His studio was in the same building that housed the original Madison Meat Market on Madison Street at Jermain Avenue. His favorite hangouts were the Black Buoy and the Corner Bar where he excelled at pool and as a teller of tales. Patti Archibald remembers, "He was a character. When my sister was getting married in 1968 I worked at the movie theater selling tickets and he used to come to the theater all the time. I said to him. "Cappy, I would like to buy one of your paintings for a wedding present for my sister, what you would see if you looked out the window from the Legion Hall toward the harbor. Would you do that? He said, 'If I need the money I will. If I don't, I won't.'"

Goat Alley Gallery opened in 1982 and was known for it's annual 725 Show, the work of artists whose Sag Harbor phone numbers began with 725. It was an ever evolving show with local artists of all ages and lasted for about twenty-five years. Artist Linda Capello remembered the gallery's owners, the late Bob and Elinor McDade, and was quoted by the *Sag Harbor Express* in Elinor's 2012 obituary. "If you

Oh, That's Another Story

The Art Shop

had a 725 phone number you were cool—part of the in crowd." The gallery was housed in the large late-Victorian building that was brought by barge from Brooklyn to Division Street, in the area still called Goat Alley.

Across a side street from the library, tucked under an enormous maple tree, is the diminutive shed called the Art Shop. In the 1950s it was the source for art supplies for artists who came here for the natural light and affordable studio space of the East End of Long Island.

Owner Gene Rhodes arrived in Sag Harbor with his family in 1947. Just after the war he had come to Noyac to go fishing with a friend and decided to move here. His son, Craig, was only five and remembers a truck piled high with all their belongings. "Someone said when they saw us coming they thought we were gypsies." Gene Rhodes first job was with R. C. Barry Hardware where he suggested they add artists' materials to their stock.

After leaving the Barrys' employ he opened the Art Shop in what had been a chicken house in the sideyard of their home. Many of the artists who frequented the shop in the 1950s are now well known and respected. "Alexander Brook and his wife, Gina Knee, Niles Spencer, Abraham Rattner, and friends

Jack and Daga Ramsay came to the shop," Craig Rhodes recalled. His father promoted the shop by starting an amateur art show and enlisting as judges famous artists and celebrities such as the movie actors Robert Montgomery and Hurd Hatfield. He also encouraged his customers to sign their names on the shop's low ceiling. Later when the property changed hands the ceiling was carefully removed and donated to the Sag Harbor Historical Society by later owners, Jeanne and Stewart Waring. Among more than 50 signatures are Alfonso Ossorio, Abraham Rattner, Robert Zoeller, Ludwig Bemelmans, Harold Davies, Sigmund Rothschild, Dick Stark, and N. Richard Nash, playwright.

Having grown up in Sag Harbor during the 1950s, Craig Rhodes has old photos of family gatherings. One in particular caught my eye, a cocktail party in the yard of their house on Main Street. The gents are in jackets and ties, and the ladies well coifed in sleeveless sheaths with proper jewels. Cocktails in hand they are living the good life, with more zest than money in the old Sag Harbor spirit.

Back when blue jeans were worn only on workdays, Sag Harbor's community was hands-on, industrious, creative, and rich in many ways now forgotten. If you needed something for dinner you took a pole and went fishing, or headed to the bay beach for mussels or clams. Vegetables were grown in most backyards and the harvest shared with friends. Even in the Great Depression and during World War II no one went hungry. And there was time for fun. There was always a rowboat to borrow, a beach within walking distance. Most important of all were the people, all different, interesting, some more flamboyant than others, someone for everyone.

If you look carefully and listen, you will find them here still.

Historical Timeline

Pre-Colonial Era: Weg-wag-onuch an Algonquin name meaning "the land at the end of the hill" is the hunting and fishing ground of Algonquian-speaking Native Americans, the Montaukett and Shinnecock tribes of hunter-gatherers (montauknation.org).

1698: An English colonist inherits a "piece of meadow," part of the marshland that covered the western portion of the future village of Sag Harbor. To the east running north to the water were three large hills, the last ending in a fifty-foot cliff at the edge of the harbor. The colonists cut into these hills and moved the sandy soil to fill in the wetlands and provide passable roads to the waterfront.

1726: Farmers from Sagaponack, the agricultural area on the Atlantic ocean, cut a road north through the woods to the harbor, which became known as Sagaponack Harbor or the Harbor of Sagg. Coastal trade develops between New England, New York, and ports to the south.

1738, 1745, 1761: Investors from Southampton divide and develop the land between Otter Pond and the harbor. Division Street running north-south marks the boundary between East Hampton and Southampton townships.

1760: Whaling from the shore was practiced by Native Americans for millennia. The first off-shore vessels leave Sag Harbor in 1760. The next year a wharf and tryworks for processing whale oil are built. This wharf is replaced in 1770 by a larger wharf called Long Wharf. In 1808 the Long Wharf is extended, and again in 1821, reaching a thousand feet to accommodate an expanding number of vessels and the burgeoning whaling trade. Warehouses, wind mills, rope walks, coopers' and boat builders' shops line the busy waterfront. Other whaling ports along the New England coast were

Oh, That's Another Story

New Bedford, Nantucket, and New London. On Long Island were Greenport, Port Jefferson, and Cold Spring Harbor.

1776: The American Revolution. Sag Harbor patriots fight in the Battle of Long Island. The victorious British military occupy Long Island for seven years, confiscate and steal supplies, food, and money. Many residents pack up as much as they can and sail for Connecticut. British blockade the harbor, stifling all trade and business. The remaining residents suffer. In 1779 Lieutenant Colonial Jonathan Meigs leads 170 men in whaleboats accompanied by two armed sloops from Guilford, Connecticut to Sag Harbor where they captured fifty-three British officers and ninety sailors, and set fire to twelve British ships which had blocked the harbor. At the end of the war, many royalists born on the East End left for England, but none from Sag Harbor.

1789: Sag Harbor is designated a port of entry by an Act of the First Congress of the United States approved by President George Washington. At the time the amount of shipping to and from Sag Harbor rivaled that of New York City. The duties and taxes collected at the Custom House by the Collector of the Port were urgently needed to finance the new republic.

1807–1812: Years after the Revolution the British continued to harass and seize American sailors, impressing them illegally to work on British ships. In an attempt to discourage this activity, Jefferson approved the Embargo Act of 1807. This impeded trade and did little to slow the advent of the War of 1812. British warships threatened Sag Harbor and were repulsed by local militia manning small canons and the village was saved.

1816: Shipping and whaling resume and continue to prosper. 1847 is the peak year of whaling in Sag Harbor. Hundreds of workers provide support for the whaling industry.

1817, 1845, 1877, 1925: Major fires in Sag Harbor fueled by wooden structures and propelled by winds off the water are economic catastrophes, barreling up Main Street until a brick building or the fledgling fire department is able to stop them. Each time the village is rebuilt, altering the historic character of the waterfront and Main Street.

1839: The first steamboat to service Sag Harbor joins the sailing fleet that provides transportation up and down Long Island Sound, to and from New England ports and New York City. By the late 1800s the sailing fleets are supplanted by steamboats, faster and powerful enough to run up rivers against the current.

1849: Whaling quickly declines, overwhelmed by three economic events. The scarcity of whales prompts extended voyages that were less and less profitable. When word of the California gold rush reaches Sag Harbor ships owners are ready to sell. In short order Sag Harbor's huge fleet and many of its men set sail for San Francisco in search of gold, leaving Long Wharf deserted. In 1859 petroleum is discovered in Pennsylvania, and cheaper, clean-burning kerosene takes the place of whale oil. In 1874 the only remaining Sag Harbor whaling ship, the *Myra*, meets her finale fate in Barbados.

Historical Timeline

1850: Manufacturing on a large scale comes to Sag Harbor. The enormous Steam Cotton Mill opens on Washington Street. Plagued by financial troubles, it burns to the ground in 1879. A steam flouring mill on the waterfront is also destroyed by fire in 1877 to be replaced by another on the same site. Oakland Brass Foundry and Clock Works is built south of the village and closes after twelve years, to be replaced by a stocking factory which lasts only three years. The stockings were followed in short order by the makers of barrel staves, the processing of Moroccan leather, and finally hats, all unsuccessful. In 1882, the buildings burned; today the site is Oakland Cemetery, the lovely oak grove where many sea captains and captains of industry are buried.

1861–1864: The Civil War. Over 300 Sag Harbor men enlist. Forty-six are killed in battle or die of their wounds. More than $2,700 is donated by townspeople in support of the Union cause.

1870: The railroad arrives at Sag Harbor, the eastern end of the line from New York City. The tracks follow the edge of the cove and end on Long Wharf. Farm produce, milk, fish, and manufactured goods now can be shipped quickly and directly to New York City and beyond. The Sag Harbor Wharf Company, owner of Long Wharf, is sold to the president of the Long Island Railroad in 1878.

1882: Fahys Watch Case Company opens a new factory on the site of the Steam Cotton Mill with 350 workers from its factory in Carlstadt, New Jersey. The company expands in 1890 to a new building on Main Street designed by New York's noted architectural firm, Carrere and Hastings. In 1911, Mr. Fahys's Alvin Silver Company moves from the main factory complex into a new building where they made silver-coated glass decanters, carafes, and perfume bottles. A fire consumes the Alvin Building in 1925. The Alvin Silver Company patterns and dies were acquired by Gorham of Providence, R.I. in 1928. Several Sag Harbor workers are hired by Gorham and move to Providence.

1887: The Ladies Village Improvement Society is established.

1891: E. W. Bliss Company begins testing torpedoes in the bay near Sag Harbor and leased space on Long Wharf for an office and machine shop.

1892: William S. Eaton, engraver with Fahys, establishes his own business manufacturing watch and clock faces. He also designs engraving machines and in 1911 forms the Engravers and Printers Machinery Company. Particularly successful is his Century Engraving Machine for jewelry and silverware. In 1918, he builds a larger work space on Jermain Avenue, that later houses Sag Harbor Industries and later still G. F. Schiavoni Plumbing and Heating, Inc.

1905: Prohibition comes early to Sag Harbor when Southampton Town decides not to renew or issue licenses to sell liquor; many saloons and hotels close their bars or go out of business. The village is dry until 1909. In 1917 the local law was changed again to allow only beer and wine in hotels. By 1920 the Volstead Act established prohibition across the country.

Oh, That's Another Story

1908: The stone breakwater to protect the harbor from nor'easter storms is completed. First requested in 1829 the appropriations needed from the US Congress were not granted until 1902. Granite for the first section is from Connecticut, the rest coming from New York City where bedrock, removed during construction of the subway, was available for free. Work can only take place during high tide. Later the inner harbor is dredged to provide a deep water channel.

1908–1910: Mrs. Russell Sage creates Pierson High School, John Jermain Memorial Library, and Mashashimuet Park in memory of her family for the benefit of Sag Harbor.

1917: World War I. The draft of that year required all men between the ages of 21 and 45 to register. Sixty-four men from Sag Harbor were chosen. Several of them served in the 77th Infantry also known as the Melting Pot Division. Its soldiers were the descendants of forty-two nationalities. Eleven local men were lost. By 1918, Sag Harbor had raised $207,000 for the cause.

1931: Fahys Watch Case Factory closes. Many skilled workers leave Sag Harbor in search of jobs. The village mayor and trustees seek another watchcase manufacturer and private donations pay for repairs to the empty factory building. Bulova Watch Company comes to Sag Harbor in 1937, creating work for 200 people.

1963: Old Whalers' Festival promotes tourism to help revive the economy.

1960s: Agawam Aircraft Products was bought by Grumman in the 1960s. Grumman built parts for the Apollo Lunar Lander in their factory on Long Wharf and closed in 1972. One factory is sold

Historical Timeline

several times over thirty years: Rowe Industries is bought by Aurora Plastics, then is purchased by Nabisco and is finally taken over by Sag Harbor Industries in 1980.

1980 After the closing of Bulova Watch Company, Croxton Collaborative designs award winning plans for rehabilitation of the factory buildings. For the next thirty years intermittent recessions, a toxic clean up, and different plans for the property are discussed by the community.

1981: Bulova Watch Company sells Sag Harbor factory. Eastville Community Historical Society is established.

1985: A new Sag Harbor Historical Society is established. Their first project: the preservation of the Umbrella House, then threatened by a condominium development. The brick structure is purported to have been fired upon by the British in the War of 1812.

1991: The Bay Street Theatre, not-for-profit regional theatre is founded.

1993: Founding of CONPOSH, an acronym for the Coalition of Neighborhoods for the Preservation of Sag Harbor. The village is divided into neighborhoods with representatives from each to communicate concerns to the rest of the community and to the village government. Public forums are held on issues that could affect the quality of life in Sag Harbor: the environment, future development, traffic, and any subject the committee found of interest. Annual New Year's Day gatherings give residents a chance to meet each other. CONPOSH is disbanded ca. 2010.

Acknowledgments

The tales in these pages were related to us by the many twentieth-century Sag Harborites who so generously sat down with us in their own homes and shared the stories of their lives. Many were born here, as early as the 1930s; others arrived in the '40s, '50s, and as late as 2000. Everyone was eager to talk, to spread the good word, and let us know that even though life has been hard, they love living here. For them Sag Harbor was and continues to be "the best place." Please understand that many of these tales have been in circulation for decades. Each time they are told they mutate, taking on the character of the teller. I have listened hard and done my best to pass on in writing what I have heard by ear.

An early interview was with May Kelman. An elegant, well-coiffed woman, she amazed us when she revealed her age. We had spent an hour or so talking about Sag Harbor the factory town, when she invited us into her kitchen for tea and cake. It was a bundt cake and delicious. Between bites, I copied the recipe from one of her cookbooks. Somewhere in the conversation she mentioned her birthday, coming up in a few days. Thinking she must be in her eighties I said, "Dare I ask your age?" "Of course," she said with a bit of pride, "I will be ninety-seven."

Invaluable to our research, Dorothy Zaykowski's *Sag Harbor, The Story of an American Beauty*, is a comprehensive survey of Sag Harbor history from the early 1700s until the 1940s, published by the Sag Harbor Historical Society. Dorothy wrote her first words on the subject in a column for the *Sag Harbor Express*, the local newspaper. One thing led to another and for the next twelve years she painstakingly gleaned early documents, frequented the history rooms of area libraries, and combed her way through

Oh, That's Another Story

a century of newspapers, along the way gaining a degree from Suffolk County Community College. The almost 400 pages of her book are packed with dates and details, revealing the depth and perseverance of her research. During the production of her book I was lucky to have the job of finding the photographs. In this process the quirky world of old Sag Harbor lodged itself in my brain. It has stayed there, percolated, and somehow, in the words of my landlady in the 1970s, Mrs. Marie Fell, "mushroomed…" Dorothy's book ended just about where ours begins and there is still the need for more fact-oriented exploration of twentieth-century local history.

Other books that I have relied on for confirming information or understanding the flavor of the times are listed in the bibliography. All of these voices have influenced and informed this work. Throughout the project, the *Sag Harbor Express* newspaper, the quintessential example of survival through hardship and affluence, has been an inspiration and a weekly reminder every Thursday.

Thank you to Catherine Creedon and Susan Mullin at the John Jermain Memorial Library for helping with the microfiche machine and accessing the Express archives.

Our thanks, too, to Denis G. Carr for his patience and care in reproducing the artwork for this book; to Dave McHugh for his expertise; to Hope Gray, Brooks Hansen, Shana Conron, and Martha Potter for their editorial assistance; and to Alison Bond for helping us understand this new age of publishing

Thanks to the following for loaning their photographs for use as reference for historical details in some of Whitney Hansen's paintings: Patricia Archibald: Sagg Harbour Coiffures; JoAnne Williams Carter: Heritage House; John Cilli: Cilli's Farm; Catherine Creedon: John Jermain Memorial Library; Ann Marino, RSHM: The Academy of the Sacred Heart of Mary; Tucker Burns Roth: Otter Hose Company; Sag Harbor Historical Society: Mrs. Eldredge's Wheelchair; Jack Youngs: Fahys Watch Case Factory, H. Klein's grocery, Schiavoni's Market, American Hotel parlor, and Sag Harbor Yacht Club.

Thanks to James Monaco for his judicious guidance in seeing this book through to the end (and for those meetings at the Corner Bar).

Thank you, Sag Harbor. It has been a pleasure.

Acknowledgments

Bibliography

Calendrille, Maryann, Ed. *Sag Harbor Is: A Literary Celebration*. Sag Harbor: Harbor Electronic Publishing, 2006.

Demos, John. *The Unredeemed Captive: A Family Story from Early America*. New York: Alfred A. Knopf, 1994.

Dierickx, Mary B. *Sag Harbor Village National Register Nomination Form*, Sag Harbor: New York State, 1994.

Eames, Alexandra. "Sag Harbor Houses," Sag Harbor: *Sag Harbor Herald*, August 16, 1990.

Logan, Robley. *Thank Ye Sag Harbor*. Mattituck, NY: Amereon House, 1987.

Mulvihill, William P. *South Fork Place Names*. Sag Harbor: Brickiln Press, 2007.

Oldenbusch, Carolyn, Ed. *Anchor to Windward: The Paintings and Diaries of Annie Cooper Boyd*. Sag Harbor Historical Society and SPLIA, 2010.

Petrow, Steven, with Richard Barons. *The Lost Hamptons*. Charleston, SC: Arcadia Publishing, 2004.

Poli, Bruce. *Suffolk County: A Place in Time*. Suffolk County, NY, 1983.

Shorto, Russell. *The Island at the Center of the World*. New York: Vintage Books, 2005.

Sleight, Harry D. *Sag Harbor in Earlier Days*. Bridgehampton, NY: The Hampton Press, 1930.

Sperling, Karen Cilli. *It's 4 a.m. Do You Know Where Your Cows Are?* Sag Harbor: private, 2007.

Tobier, Nina, Ed. *Voices of Sag Harbor: A Village Remembered*. Sag Harbor: Harbor Electronic Publishing, 2007.

Wright, Michael. "Sag Harbor Home to One of the Oldest Black Second-Home Communities." Southampton, NY: *Southampton Press*, Feb. 22, 2012.

Zaykowski, Dorothy Ingersoll. *Sag Harbor, The Story of an American Beauty*. Sag Harbor Historical Society, 1991.

Zaykowski, Dorothy Ingersoll. *The Old Burying Ground at Sag Harbor, NY*. Westminster, MD: Heritage Books, 2003.

About the Author

Alexandra Eames, author, bought an 1894 Sag Harbor house with her husband Chris Leonard in 1977. An interior designer, she also wrote for a local newspaper, published several books on design, and styled interiors for magazines. A founding member of the Sag Harbor Historical Society she worked on the extension of the local historic district, is a member of the board of Mashashimuet Park and the Sag Harbor Tree Fund. Now retired, she spends most of her time in Sag Harbor with trips to Vermont where she and her husband are restoring a 200-year-old Federal brick house.

About the Artist

Whitney Hansen, artist, came to Sag Harbor in 1965. Her subjects are varied, from still life and portrait to seascapes and landscapes. The medium is oil and makes use of the woodcut process on textured rice paper. After the print is pulled, the surface detail is hand-painted in oil. Her works are in the collections of the Metropolitan Museum of Art, New York, the Scripps College Museum in Claremont, CA, and the Bowdoin College Museum in Brunswick, ME.

Made in the USA
Middletown, DE
28 June 2015